A family history
Bloodline

Lynne Cohen

BLOODLINE: A FAMILY HISTORY

Lynne Cohen

Order this book online at www.trafford.com
or email orders@trafford.com

Most Trafford titles are also available at major online book retailers.

Printed in the United States of America.

ISBN: 978-1-4269-7557-8 (sc)
ISBN: 978-1-4269-7558-5 (e)

Trafford rev. 09/22/2011

 www.trafford.com

North America & international
toll-free: 1 888 232 4444 (USA & Canada)
phone: 250 383 6864 ◆ fax: 812 355 4082

Dedicated to:
Martin Jay Cohen, my beloved brother of blessed memory

TABLE OF CONTENTS

INTRODUCTION

This book began as an introduction to my autobiography, but it quickly took on a life of its own. In the summer of 2007, the more I researched my recent ancestors, the more I needed to know about these remarkable people. The story became far too long for an introduction, so I decided to write two volumes, well three actually. As I became more familiar with my family's background in the Maritimes, as I learned about the gruesome double murder of my great aunt and uncle that took place in Glace Bay, Nova Scotia, in 1941 – right about the time dozens of my other relatives were being slaughtered in Europe – it became increasingly clear to me I needed to write about those horrifying Maritime killings too. We'll see.

Before going on, it must be noted that one of my first cousins, Judith Kalin, as well as her husband Dr. David Kalin, devoted countless hours putting together a family tree for their son Michael's bar mitzvah in 1984. So comprehensive was their project that it ended up providing every basic piece of evidence for *Bloodline: A Family History*. In fact, it is all but certain that I would not have been able to begin my project without the loving and hard work of my cousins. For her side of the family, Judy and

David produced a six-and-a-half-foot long by ten-inch wide document that covers the names, birth dates, marriages, divorces, professions and, where pertinent, the deaths of more than 200 family members. Judy and David also made a similarly huge family tree of the Kalins, as well as of each of Judy's and David's mother's sides, the Levin and Sherman families respectively.

Also important is the fact that all of the Cohens in my family left Russia as Kekons. Once in Canada, the younger Kekons changed their name to Cohen. Why? The exact reason is lost to history, but the answer probably has something to do with the Kekon's irrational belief that Cohen sounded more Canadian.

My job here is to flesh out parts of the Cohen family tree. But because of the amount of work involved, unfortunately, not even ten percent of the family is discussed. A portion of the Cohen family tree, however, is reproduced on page xii and xiii to help you keep track of just about everyone mentioned in the following chapters.

In May 2010, I made a presentation to the Ottawa Jewish Historical Society on my family's history. By all accounts the talk was a huge success. About fifty Ottawans – and a couple of friends from Chelsea, Quebec – came and listened to a shortened version of *Bloodline: A Family History*. Everyone seemed to love the stories of the Cohen family. Almost all my cousins – and my sister Barbara Cohen-Colllier – participated in preparing the talk by sending me personal, priceless anecdotes and other information about their parents. Whatever had to be cut for the talk for time purposes is included here in Chapter Six.

A note on the text: In memoirs like this one where much is known yet much is still obscure, it is tempting to add phrases such as "They might have attended such and such a school," or "They could have travelled by ship and train." But as seasoned readers know, too much of this makes for tedious prose. Though I have certainly used the terms "probably" and "possibly," to avoid a surfeit of them, I have made some assumptions for which I take full responsibility, and I invite my critics to forgive me for favouring a good read over academic meticulousness.

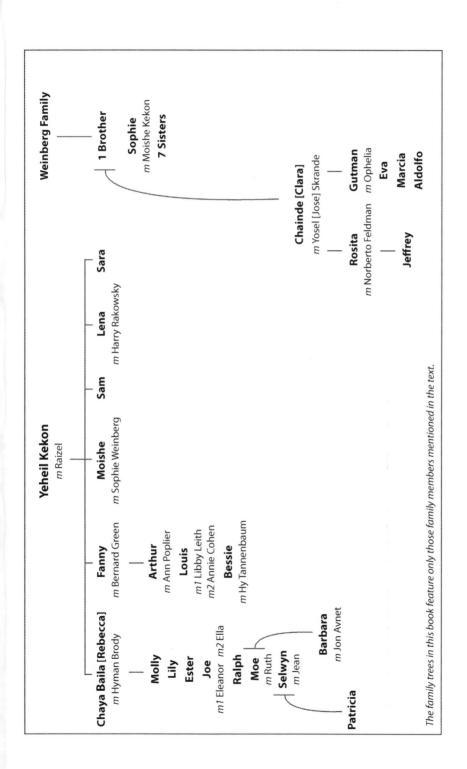

Weinberg Family

1 Brother

Sophie
m Moishe Kekon

7 Sisters

Chainde [Clara]
m Yosel [Jose] Skrande

Rosita
m Norberto Feldman

Gutman
m Ophelia

Jeffrey

Eva
Marcia
Aldolfo

Yeheil Kekon
m Raizel

Moishe
m Sophie Weinberg

Sam

Lena
m Harry Rakowsky

Sara

Chaya Baila [Rebecca]
m Hyman Brody

Fanny
m Bernard Green

Arthur
m Ann Poplier

Louis
m1 Libby Leith m2 Annie Cohen

Bessie
m Hy Tannenbaum

Molly
Lily
Ester
Joe
m1 Eleanor m2 Ella

Ralph

Moe
m Ruth

Selwyn
m Jean

Barbara
m Jon Avnet

Patricia

The family trees in this book feature only those family members mentioned in the text.

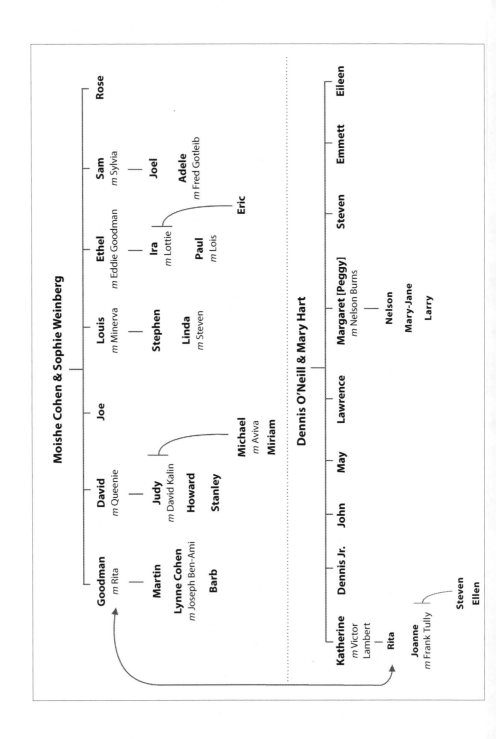

Moishe Cohen & Sophie Weinberg

Goodman
m Rita

David
m Queenie

Joe

Louis
m Minerva

Ethel
m Eddie Goodman

Sam
m Sylvia

Rose

Martin

Judy
m David Kalin

Howard

Stanley

Stephen

Linda
m Steven

Ira
m Lottie

Paul
m Lois

Joel

Adele
m Fred Gotleib

Lynne Cohen
m Joseph Ben-Ami

Barb

Michael
m Aviva

Miriam

Eric

Dennis O'Neill & Mary Hart

Katherine
m Victor Lambert

Dennis Jr.

John

May

Lawrence

Margaret [Peggy]
m Nelson Burns

Steven

Emmett

Eileen

Rita

Joanne
m Frank Tully

Nelson

Mary-Jane

Larry

Steven

Ellen

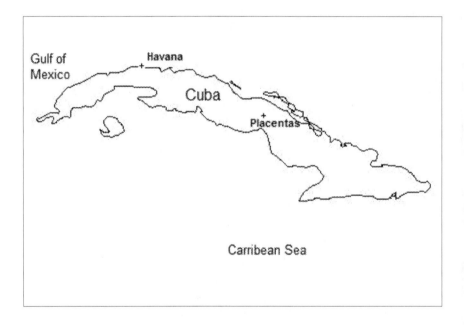

Gulf of
Mexico

Havana

Cuba

Placentas

Carribean Sea

CHAPTER ONE:
The Kekons Come to Canada

Pogroms, poverty and oppression had taken their toll. His beloved wife Raizel, who had lovingly borne Yeheil Kekon six healthy children, finally died of her lingering illness, maybe cancer, maybe pneumonia, maybe tuberculosis. There is no record. She was not yet fifty-five. For Yeheil, fifty-seven, my great grandfather, the time had come to depart the Motherland and take the rest of his children to join their three siblings who had already left Russia and settled in North America.

Born in the middle of the nineteenth century in a tiny Russian *shtetl* – somewhere in centuries old Lithuania – Yeheil Kekon was making the final preparations to get out from under the Russian Tsar. He gave the last bribery instalment of five hundred rubles to the corrupt local official, who hastily handed him the emigration papers for himself, his thirteen-year-old son Sam, his younger daughter Lena and my grandfather-to-be Moishe, about nineteen at the time. It was 1902.

Jews lived in Lithuania as long ago as the eighth century and, in significant numbers, since the fourteenth century. Sixteen hundred years ago they were invited to live in the muddy, foggy, hilly land on the eastern shore of the Baltic Sea by Lithuania's resourceful nation builders – Augustus II and Augustus III – who knew great business people when they encountered them. Resourceful as always, Jews also established themselves as critical to Lithuanian diplomacy and defence. Moreover, throughout those centuries, the Jewish community – as it was wont to do – proved itself resilient, as the Lithuanian empire endured wars and turbulence amid stretches of tottery peaceful existence.

In 1795, an alliance between Prussia and Austria on the one side and Russia on the other ended the independence of Poland, and at the same time Lithuania became a large province of Russia. Two uprisings by the Poles failed, and thus ended Polish influence on the Lithuanian way of life. Now only under Russian predominance and Tsarist rule, Lithuania abided severe and restrictive regimes, but such authoritative cruelty failed to obliterate Jewish culture and language.

In my mind's eye, Yeheil – who never travelled to larger Lithuanian cities like Vilnius or Kaunas – came from a community not unlike the tiny rural village, or *shtetl,* portrayed in the classic movie *Fiddler on the Roof.* About seventy-five large Jewish families lived in small, wooden, rickety homes in a space the size of half a Canadian football field. The main road – not much more than a thirty-five-foot wide dirt lane – accommodated the crucial businesses, such as the butcher, the tailor and the blacksmith, and provided the rutty path for the horse-drawn milk trucks. The small indistinctive synagogue occupied one end of the road where many of the town's men met for prayer three times a day and study sessions in the late evenings.

In leaving his ramshackle village, Yeheil was joining a mass exodus. Between 1881 and 1914 nearly two million Jews would arrive in the United States and Canada from Eastern Europe. Of Russia's original five million Jews, this was not an insignificant number.

They could barely contain their excitement. Leaving from the port of Kaliningrad on the Baltic Sea, or maybe Gdansk, the Kekons traveled by train and by foot from their *shtetl* to the waiting ocean liner. Wearing their Sabbath clothes (long pants and button down shirts on the males and a drab peasant dress on Lena) and their worn but durable leather shoes, the bedraggled group of four – each carrying a small suitcase stuffed with their favourite belongings, the few things they simply could not leave behind – advanced to the huge port nearest their ancient village.

Though modern, and possibly even new, the high powered steamship they took to Halifax was anything but comfortable. A Cunard Line or Allen ship, it was crowded with some nine-hundred anxious souls, each of whom had paid the equivalent of about two-hundred and fifty dollars (though young children sailed for free) for the dangerous journey. A small proportion of the travelers went first class, but the Kekons crowded into the steerage section, where they all bunked together – with other relatively poor families – in a small cabin near the bottom of the ship.

The twenty-day voyage offered little in the way of rest or diversion. Even on sunny days, the upper deck was too populated for enjoyment, and the runny, wet slop that was offered as food three times daily was edible only because it was necessary.

Exhausted, the four Kekons were thrilled and relieved to alight at Halifax Harbour. Today Canadians would likely call these ragged east coast arrivals refugees, and would probably soon hand them everything to make their lives easy and improve their health. In 1902, they were poor immigrants who filed one by one into a shed at Pier Two at the north end of the harbour. They were questioned, registered and shuffled through. But they were eligible for absolutely nothing except landing rights (provided they were healthy), eventual citizenship and freedom from tyranny, which of course were not small gifts. Only those heading to farm in Western Canada were given free land by the Canadian government.

Happy, finally, to be on shore the Kekons rested for a few hours before making the final leg of their journey to Nova Scotia's far eastern coast, the least popular route for Jews arriving in Canada. Though a promising and popular place for would-be coal miners arriving from Europe and the Caribbean, Glace Bay attracted fewer Jews than the established, high density cities did. Most who arrived in Halifax took the train to Montreal or Toronto. The Kekons, like their family members before them, made their way, also by train, to Cape Breton, then all the way to the craggy shores of Glace Bay.

Baie de Glace (Ice Bay) was originally settled by the French in about 1720 in order to supply a nearby fortress with coal. After the Dominion Coal Company was established in 1893, and more mines opened in and around the town, the population grew. In 1901, when the Town of Glace Bay was incorporated – about the time Yeheil and his children arrived – the population was just under seven-thousand.

Finally in the New World, Yeheil was excited to see his daughters Chaya Baila and Fanny who had arrived in 1895. Shortly after settling, Yeheil made arrangements to visit his oldest daughter Sara, who had moved to New York. Lena and Sam, who had travelled with Yeheil across the Atlantic, would also move to the Big Apple a few years after arriving in Canada.

It might be an exaggeration to call turn of the century Glace Bay a thriving Jewish community, but it was slowly becoming a small, bustling Jewish centre. By 1927 some ninety Jewish families – many of them quite large – had settled in the coastal town, which had grown to a total population of more than twenty thousand. Only several years on, the Glace Bay Jewish community began its slow decline. Virtually every Jewish child from the area grew up and left the rural coastal town for Canadian or American city life. In recent years, the local Orthodox synagogue (and the fist in Canada) that opened in 1901 – Congregation Sons of Israel – was often not even able to attract a Sabbath minion, which is ten men, the minimum number for a formal prayer session. By 2010, the one-hundred and nine-year-old synagogue had closed.

Upon arriving in Canada, several of Yeheil's children legally changed their last name to Cohen, though he himself kept the name Kekon, which appears on his tombstone in the tiny Glace Bay Jewish cemetery. The name change was probably an effort to become more "Canadian" and thus be accepted by the locals. Those locals happened to be the tough coal miners of Cape Breton Island.

At the time, Cape Breton coal was needed everywhere in Canada. It was a period of great expansion across the country – factories, shipbuilding, trains, steel mills, etc. – and Glace Bay rose to the challenge. The Dominion Coal Company advertised throughout the world, even offering free passage to those willing to do the grinding, dirty work under the surface of the land. Indeed, before the turn of the century, every day Glace Bay gained hundreds of newcomers, increasing its population from several hundred to eight-thousand very quickly, within a few years.

The arriving Jews were not interested in mine work. It just wasn't in their blood. They had little experience with such back-breaking work. They were anxious, however, to provide all the surrounding services, such as apartments for rent, general store goods, door to door sales of rags and other household objects, teaching and administrative work.

Yeheil, like many poor Jews of his day, was well educated in Jewish law. Known proudly in his Russian *shtetl* as a *yeshiva bocher* in his youth, he learned Jewish law from the ancient texts, including the Talmud and Torah, in a small run-down school for such learning for five years between the ages of eleven and sixteen. Despite such elite Jewish training, Yeheil ended up not terribly observant when he came to Canada, for reasons unknown. Like many of the hundreds of thousands of North American Jews of his time, he likely found survival difficult enough without the extra "burdens" involved in performing Jewish rituals. The G-d-given tasks are many, expensive and time-consuming, among them: eating only kosher food; observing the twenty-five-hour Sabbath without participating in commerce; and, for men, praying three times every day for a minimum total of approximately forty-five minutes.

The long term consequences of his abandoning religious observance are widespread and profound: most of his progeny are not religious either, and many of them have almost completely abandoned Jewish practice or have children who intermarried with non-Jews. Yet, generations hence, some members of his family – like tens of thousands of Jews in late twentieth century North America – have come back to a Torah way of life from very far away, indeed.

Yeheil died in 1913 at the age of 72. He proudly spent part of his later days living in a small shack on Glace Bay's Brookside Street, until his daughter and her husband, Fanny and Bernard Green, convinced him to live out his last days with them, in their small home with their four children. Speaking of my great aunt Fanny, her immediate family started what quickly became an impressive tradition among Cohen descendants and their extended families: becoming lawyers and doctors. Though not unusual for Jewish families of that era to spawn such professionals, I have always been proud of the sheer number among our relatives. Since Fanny's eldest son Dr. Arthur Green – who happened to be the first Jewish child born in Glace Bay in1899 – trained at Halifax's Dalhousie University in the 1920s, my family has produced or welcomed into the fold more than fifteen physicians, including a couple of innovative and well-known New York dentists but not including a genetics professor and a few clinical psychologists. The number of lawyers – some of whom could not make it into medical school – is also about fifteen.

Chaya Baila was the first of Yeheil's children to flee the brutality of Tsar Nicolas II. Wanting to make friends in her adopted country, she quickly changed her name to Rebecca. She arrived in Glace Bay in 1895 and soon after married Hyman Brody, the first Jew to land in Glace Bay in 1890. They ran a town grocery store and owned property. They rented out apartments. Before this pioneering woman and her animal-loving husband were mercilessly murdered in their kitchen in 1941, they managed to raise seven children, including Molly – reportedly a child from Hyman's first marriage – Lily, Esther, Joe (born in 1900), Ralph, Moe (born in 1910) and Selwyn.

Rebecca's younger brother, Moishe, or Morris as he was later called in Canada, was my grandfather, though I never met him. He died at the age of seventy in 1952, while my father was studying medicine at Montreal's McGill University.

A few years after the Kekons arrived in Glace Bay, a traditional *shidoch* (or match-making) was arranged for Moishe. Rebecca's in-laws in New York City introduced him to my grandmother, eighteen-year-old Sophie Weinberg, who had arrived in the United States three years earlier from Bialystok, Russia. At fifteen, she crossed the Atlantic Ocean alone to New York to work for the Brody family as an au pair.

In 1900, the town of Bialystok, a textile-based city made up mostly of Jews – about sixty-three percent of the total population of sixty-six thousand – belonged to Russia, having passed to the massive country after the Peace of Tilsit in 1807. The city passed into different hands over the later decades, eventually falling to both the Nazis and the Russians during World War Two.

CHAPTER TWO:
Sophie and Many Tears

Sophie's immediate family traveled two hundred miles to see her off in 1901 from the same Baltic Sea port that Yeheil and his children – including Moishe, who was to eventually become her husband – would depart from one year later.

Crying uncontrollably, Sophie slowly climbed aboard the crowded steam ship that was to take her three thousand miles to New York City. The brave girl waved her small, tear-soaked handkerchief to seven sisters, one brother and both parents. Then she began the slow, nauseating voyage to a new life.

As Sophie said good bye to her immediate family, she was also saying goodbye forever to virtually all of her many aunts, uncles, cousins and other relatives who lived in and around what is now essentially Jew-free Bialystok, Poland. Before the Germans occupied the city for the last time in 1941 – they had transferred it to the Soviets after a brief occupation in September 1939, as per the Soviet-German pact – Bialystok (total population by that time three-hundred-fifty-thousand) was a thriving Jewish community with fifty-thousand members. True, the Jews were no longer more than half the total population and, yes, the city had a lot of dirty, industrial age poverty. But Bialystok also had a huge central synagogue, some three-hundred textile mills built and run by enterprising Jews, and many modern schools for Jewish children.

By the time the Nazis were finished with the place, two-thousand of the town's Jews had been forced into and burnt alive in the main synagogue; thirty-three-hundred men – many considered Jewish intelligentsia – were murdered at a field right outside town; one-thousand Jews were rounded up and killed on the spot as the final liquidation of Bialystok began in February 1943; and the rest, about forty-thousand Jews, were soon deported to the Treblinka and Majdanek death camps.

Sophie lost some eighty members of her family (my family) to the murderous Nazis. I like to think at least some of them – made of the super strong character and willpower that came with Sophie to New York and eventually to Nova Scotia – were members of the Bialystok resistance. Though less well known and fewer in number than the unbending fighters of the Warsaw Ghetto uprising, the seventy-two members of the Bialystok underground held off the Nazis for almost a month with very few weapons and by constantly changing hiding places. The last two resisters in the ghetto committed suicide, but a few dozen apparently escaped and joined the partisans. Maybe some were members of my family.

CHAPTER THREE:
Cuba and the Skrandes

Take a detour in space and time. My grandmother Sophie's brother, whose first name and age are not known by anyone I know, married somewhere in what is today Poland, and he and his wife had several children, including a daughter Chainda Weinberg in 1905. Chainda was a beautiful girl, but more than that she had a beautiful singing voice, and all of her friends and family loved to hear it. Later in life, as her beauty gently and naturally faded, a profound sadness took hold and swelled. Living in Cuba with her husband and children, she came to realize why her parents and siblings had stopped writing letters: her entire family – all except her Aunt Sophie in Nova Scotia – had been massacred by the Nazis.

Chainda's daughter Rosita Skrande, who was born in Cuba in 1933, explains that her mother – who was given the name "Clara" by Cuban officials as she entered the island in the mid 1920s – never recovered psychologically after learning of her European family's horrific fate. "My mother would not talk about her past," says Rosita, who now lives in Maryland, and who refuses – because of the 1959 communist revolution – to ever return to her beloved Cuba. "After the Second World War, my mother would not sing, not ever again. I did not want to upset my mother more, so I almost never asked about her family in Poland, though I was curious."

Scraps of Chainda's life in small town Poland can be determined through a few surviving details and more than a couple of rumours. She eventually married Yosel Skrande who, tales are told, couldn't get enough time with his darling Chainda during the days before their wedding. "We used to hear stories about how my dad would secretly cross the river at night to go to Chainda's section of the town," says Rosita, whose devoted and good-humoured husband Norberto died in 2008. "There, the two of them would join gatherings of young people and have a good time. Sometimes my mother would sing for the entire group."

After Chainda and Yosel were married in the early 1920s, Yosel alone took a steamship to North America. "It was their dream, like almost every Jew's, to escape Poland," says Rosita, "even at that time years before official Nazism. Poland was full of anti-Semitism and many Jews lived in ghetto-like communities. To them, America had streets paved with gold."

Yosel wanted to find a job or business and a home in America before he sent for Chainda. But because of U.S. quotas for Jewish immigrants at the time, he was not allowed to enter the country. Disappointed, he ended up going to Cuba. At the point of entry, Cuban authorities quickly changed his name to Jose, a perfect Spanish name to suit his new homeland. "The officials wrote the names that were easiest for them," says Rosita. "Yosel was his Yiddish name. The Cuban authorities were not going to trouble themselves with that language so they wrote Jose. That happened with all immigrants. They were not going to fool around with spelling. All the Jewish people in Cuba have Spanish names."

Jose – thinking he and his wife would only stay a few years in Cuba – settled himself down in the tiny town of Placentas where he set up a small dry goods store that also sold clothing. Almost immediately, he realized he had found paradise. After one year, he decided it was time for Chainda to come see for herself. He sent her the money to travel to be with him. Upon arrival, she also fell in love with the island. Like Jose, she deeply appreciated its golden beaches and freedom from bigotry. And upon entering the island, Cuban officials bestowed on her the new name Clara.

Jose and Clara soon had a son, Gutman, in 1926, and seven years later Rosita was born. Interestingly, Gutman was born only four years after my father Goodman, who was born in Reserve Mines, Nova Scotia in 1922. They were second cousins. Gutman is Goodman in Yiddish, the language of the Jews in Eastern Europe and Russia for hundreds and hundreds of years. Like Goodman, Gutman was named after Sophie's grandfather, who would be my great, great grandfather.

It cannot be stressed enough how important letters were in those days to connect people overseas, nor how much of an impact the missives suddenly stopping had on the mental health of the recipients. My family was no exception. Faithfully, in Yiddish, Clara wrote to her family in Europe and to her Aunt Sophie in Nova Scotia every week. Writing was a kind of desperate connection – Clara's only connection – to the past she left behind and the family she dearly missed. Loyally, her family members wrote back, chatty letters about the weather, the harvests, business, who was marrying, new babies, and who died. Clara lovingly devoured news about her large extended family back in the old country.

Did my Jewish relatives in Poland write about politics and the worsening anti-Semitism on the continent? According to my father Goodman, surprisingly, no. Despite the clamouring of increasing numbers of desperate Jews in Europe trying to get into Canada – and being rejected by the federal government under Prime Minister Mackenzie King virtually wholesale – my family for some reason never tried, nor even complained, at least in the letters.

Abruptly, sometime in early 1940 – several months after the Nazi invasion of Poland in the late summer of 1939 – the letters stopped. From reading the newspapers – and even from their own experiences before leaving Poland – Clara and Jose were aware of the intensifying bigotry toward Jews through much of Europe. They and Sophie knew about the legalized anti-Semitism in Germany, well before the Nazis marched into and overwhelmed half of Poland. (The northern half was for a time being run by the Russians, who were certainly vicious and cruel, but not as evil as the Nazis. In fact, the Russians offered hope for Polish Jews who fled to the north.)

But, like most Jews who were actually living under the Nazi hatred, Clara, Jose and Sophie did not believe the Germans would do more than decree, temporarily, increasingly scandalous and dangerous but also ridiculous and irritating social and economic restrictions against them. Though the new anti-Semitism was terrifying in scope, such hatred had been an every day part of life for Jews for centuries. It was scarier than normal, but it was never surprising, and not usually fatal. In 1941, despite some evidence of the impending Holocaust, and despite widespread knowledge of European Jews being "transported east," no one in North America believed the war would end with the annihilation of more than half of all Europe's Jews.

As my father Goodman often recalled with emotion decades later, soon after the letters stopped, his mother in Nova Scotia and her cousin in Cuba became very frightened indeed. They tried to imagine something innocuous. Maybe the postage became too expensive? Ridiculous. Maybe the letters were being stolen by the postal employees? Not likely. Could the family be in trouble and not able to write? G-d help them!

When they learned the stark truth after the war's end, Clara experienced a kind of shock from which she never recovered. "My mother was traumatized," says Rosita. "It was terrible. She could not speak about what had happened." Sophie, who was by then a full forty-four years removed from Europe – compared with Clara's fifteen years – did not suffer the same degree of shock and trauma as did her niece. Sophie, however, did grieve for years.

But life had to move on. Like his parents Clara and Jose – who moved their family to Havana in the early 1950s – Gutman loved his native Cuba. The weather was almost tropical, the beaches were white and gorgeous and at least some kind of freedom – under authoritarian capitalist Fulgencio Batista – reigned. Gutman loved Cuba so much that, after he grew up and became a successful accountant, he threw his financial and political support behind an old school chum, Fidel Castro, a young lawyer trying to overthrow the undemocratic Batista. I well remember my own parents Goodman and Rita telling me how they also had, along with my Uncle Dave and on Gutman's say so, sent money to the revolutionaries in the late 1950s to support Castro's "worthy cause."

Around that time, Uncle Dave – my father Goodman's next older sibling by four years – did some very unusual travelling. After the war, most people – including my own parents – pretty much ignored distant relatives they had never met, and concentrated on building their own young families, communities and careers. Uncle Dave, on the other hand, with a new business and young family, decided to travel to Cuba in 1953 to meet his first cousin Clara and her family. He went to Cuba with a local Ottawa baseball team, but really, explains Rosita, "Dave came to Cuba because he was a very caring person. My mother, if she had won the lottery, she would not have been as happy. She and my father were so thrilled to meet him. He became very close to us. He came to my wedding, my son's bar mitzvah and my daughter's wedding in America."

Of course, after the successful 1959 Cuban revolution, things did not turn out as hoped. "For a period of time Castro tried to appear as a good and decent leader," says Rosita. "Castro had not declared himself a communist but he was instituting some policies that made us know he was. He lied to everyone.

"By the way, I believe Castro survived for so many years thanks to Canada. That is what I dislike about Canada. Canadians supported him.

I refuse to ever return to Cuba. My son Jeffrey's synagogue organized a trip to Havana in 2005 and he begged me to come and show him around. I refused. For some reason, Jeffrey never went."

Around 1960, my Uncle Dave generously sent more money to Cuba, this time to help Gutman and his family flee the island and move to the U.S. Rosita and her husband Norberto were already settled in Silver Spring, Maryland, near Washington D.C. Now everyone else in the family fled: Gutman, his wife Ophelia, their three children, and his parents Clara and Jose. Like much of the upper crust of Cuban society, they got out in 1961, a short time before the borders were permanently closed. "The professionals, the cream of society, were the first to leave when it was discovered what a liar Castro was," explains Rosita. For the rest who wanted to leave later, it was too late.

Gutman and his parents hated leaving. "They were all really homesick for Cuba, especially my brother Gutman and our mother Clara," says Rosita. "It really was a wonderful country. Not perfect. There was some corruption, but before Castro it was beautiful and free. You were able to do what you wanted. Nature was beautiful and the beaches were gorgeous."

In America, Clara – already permanently scarred emotionally by the Holocaust – struggled even more. "My parents came to live with me in Maryland," explains Rosita, who cared for Clara for about 13 years until she died in 1974. "My mother had such a hard time. My parents had to leave everything behind in Cuba. They came to the United States with the bare minimum. They spoke no English. My father got used to life here, and he got a job. But my mother never did. "

Rosita was lucky in that she knew English before she left Cuba in the late 1950s. "I had gone to an American school in Cuba," she says. "Why did I do that? When I finished high school I went to Havana University to study pharmacy, which I hated. When the political strife started the university was closed. My mom said 'You are not going to be sitting here watching television all day.' So I enrolled in an American school and when I graduated from there I spoke English. I even started teaching in the school."

In the U.S., Rosita's brother Gutman and his wife Ophelia – who had two daughters, Eva and Marcia, and a son Aldolfo – also struggled. Living in Miami, Gutman never completely recovered from his home sickness. Nor did he recover financially. Unable to work as an accountant, he tried being a businessman, but was not very successful. Thankfully, Aldolfo succeeded brilliantly in business in America. "He was phenomenally accomplished as a clothing manufacturer, and he ended up supporting most of his family, including his parents," explains my first cousin Judy Kalin.

As a direct result of his experiences in Cuba, Gutman viscerally hated communism, while he deeply loved freedom and democracy. So it is with irony and passion that he frequently argued in the early 1970s with my cousin by marriage Fred Gottlieb, at the time a mid-thirty-something-year-old genetics professor at Penn State University. "It is sort of hilarious to remember them debating at my brother Stanley's bar mitzvah," says Judy, about the September 2, 1972 event. Here was Fred, she explains, the highly-educated liberal-minded professor – living freely in the greatest democracy in the world – arguing in *favour* of communism as an inevitable and progressive way of the future. And on the other side of the debate was Gutman Skrande, who barely escaped his beloved Cuba with the shirt on his back, strenuously defending his new country – where success had eluded him – and fiercely denouncing communism.

Sadly, Gutman – madly loved even by his communist-sympathizing relatives in both Canada and the United States – died at age fifty-five of a bad heart, obviously a broken heart. "It was absolutely tragic," says Judy, who adored him. Not too many years later, his wife Ophelia, not exactly emotionally stable at the best of times, died tragically when she fell asleep while smoking. Her lit cigarette started a fire in the chair.

Interestingly, Rosita clearly remembers one crazy visit to one of her dearest cousins – my dad's sister Ethel and her husband Eddie Goodman, in Queens, New York – in 1955 or 1956. (Clearly, it is only a fun coincidence that their last name is the exactly the same as my father's first). Rosita describes the trip: "The very next day after I arrived in New York, Eddie and Ethel bundled me into their car, and we drove all the way to Ottawa. It was about nine hours, but we just had to go. All of Ethel's siblings – including Goodman – lived in Ottawa and she was anxious for me to meet them." By this time, Rosita had only met David and Ethel.

"When we finally arrived in Ottawa, I met your Aunt Rose and your uncles Joe, Sam and Lou," says Rosita. "I met all their kids too. I saw your dad, Goodman, but not as much as the others. He was very busy as a young doctor.

"We also phoned Sophie, who was still in Nova Scotia," Rosita continues. "I was very sad that I did not get to meet her." Sophie was finishing up business with the general store and the house in Reserve Mines, selling the property and getting ready to move to Ottawa herself.

CHAPTER FOUR:
Life in Reserve and the Bay

There was nothing unusual at the turn of the nineteenth century in Jewish "girls" marrying in their mid teens. This was certainly the rule in my family. For instance, Fanny Green's first child Arthur was born when she was only sixteen or seventeen. The young ladies in those days were known to have the needed physical and mental prowess to raise lots of children and run a household, even a business if necessary. One hundred years ago, most children grew up fast, and they took their responsibilities seriously.

Sophie's original plans were to start a new life in New York by first spending time as an au pair, looking after the children of a New York family, the Brodys. She planned to later find a husband and settle down in the Big Apple, even then the international centre of modern Jewish life. But things worked out differently, as they often do.

Glace Bay's Rebecca Kekon – married to Hyman Brody (of the New York family) who had moved to Nova Scotia in 1895 – realized, after living near her brother Moishe for four years since he arrived from Russia in 1902, that he was indeed ready to marry. In New York, Sophie was also of marrying age. The fix was in. The New York Brody's arranged with the Glace Bay Brody's for the two to meet. The meeting went well. They married in 1906. She was 19. He was 23.

Sophie happily left New York City to settle down and raise a family in the considerably less cosmopolitan Glace Bay. To be completely accurate, they bought a relatively cheap place a few miles outside Glace Bay, in the mining village of Reserve Mines, current population only about 2,100. It may sound unimportant in this day of universal amalgamation, but at a 2001 reunion of the some four-hundred Jews who left Glace Bay and of their family members, the Cohen descendants were heartily teased about being "outsiders." Coming originally from Reserve, did we really belong at a reunion of the Bay crowd?

As they were growing up in Reserve Mines, Nova Scotia, in the early 1900s, the members of my family certainly never imagined the horrific events that would happen to their relatives both in the Maritimes and in Europe in the decades to come. They were preoccupied with their hardscrabble lives in the rural town, helping each other and the struggling coal miners who were their neighbours and customers at the general store they ran.

Enough cannot be said about the phenomenal strength, energy and innate business sense of Sophie Cohen. Moreover, from all accounts, she was also an excellent cook, according to my cousin Judy who spent summers in Reserve with her brother Howard and with some Ottawa and New York cousins before I was born.

Moishe, like his father Yeheil, loved to learn Torah and Talmud. So while Sophie ran the general store – on credit as it turned out, as her customers never had much money – while she baked daily in her own family oven enough of her famously delicious and popular cakes to sell to just about the entire town; while she weekly beheaded and plucked chickens she bred in the back yard coop; while she milked the family's cow and fed the horse every morning before anyone got up; while she cared in every wifely and motherly way for her husband and their growing energetic brood of five boys and two girls; and while she scrubbed her small house and outhouse until they sparkled; Cape Breton legend has it that he, Moishe, simply sat all day and learned. When Moishe wasn't studying

Jewish law, he was learning English by reading newspapers, particularly the sports sections.

His exercise breaks consisted of taking the family's two Border Collies for walks up and down the only major street in Reserve, stepping high with his walking stick, smiling and waving at all his neighbours, as if he had not a care in world.

Non-religious though he was, he looked and sometimes acted the part of the observant Jew. For one thing, Sophie tried her best to keep a kosher kitchen (though of course her butchering her own chickens was a problem in this regard). Moishe grew his beard, studied Talmud all day most days, and walked five miles every Sabbath to the Glace Bay synagogue, Sons of Israel, and back home in time for lunch.

As mentioned, Sophie and Moishe had seven children, five boys and two girls. My dad was the youngest, born August 28, 1922, about 16 years after the oldest, his sister Rose, born in 1906. Following Rose there was a child every two years, until Joe, then four years later David and then four years after that my dad, Goodman. According to my cousins in-the-know, Goodman was the favourite of everyone, all the time. From the time he was a baby, when he got all the attention, right through high school, when he got all the praise and encouragement, to the time he went to university, when he got all the extra money.

Goody was unbelievably cute. Like his six older siblings, he was born in the house behind the Reserve Mines general store that his parents owned and his mother ran. Unlike his older siblings, and apparently because he was so adorable, he breast fed until he was a full four years old. This well-guarded family secret lasted until Goody died in 1990, when word started to spill out that, despite everyone's best efforts, they could not get the determined little boy to stop breast feeding.

Jon Avnet is a Hollywood movie producer – and Rebecca and Hyman Brody's grandson-in-law – who has so far put together more than 30 major big screen productions, including Fried Green Tomatoes. He wrote – as part of the eulogy of his uncle-in-law Joseph Brody – as clear a depiction of life in the Bay area as any I have read. Avnet said that life in Glace Bay and Reserve in the early part of the last century was "cold and harsh." Almost everyone was poor, and fist fighting was a way of life. On Saturday nights, the dance floor above the Brody's general store in Glace Bay was the scene of local coal miners drinking away their problems, and then fighting until the sun came up. Lots of the younger boys in town fought each other in the street after school, usually the Catholics beating up the Jews, but from Avnet's understanding, "some of the Jews gave pretty good too."

According to Avnet, my father's first cousin Joseph Brody "was big and strong and was the toughest kid in town and a Jew at the same time paradoxically." In the 1996 eulogy, Avnet said: "Joe Brody didn't start fights, but he did finish them. In the rabid anti-semitism of his time, you had to fight or you would be beat."

Only once, continued Avnet, did Joe Brody lose a fight: "Three older kids jumped him and beat him badly. When he recovered, he tracked down one of the boys, and wreaked his revenge. He found the second and did the same. The story goes that the third fellow left town. The third one was smart. No one fought with Joe after that."

All the children of the Bay (and Reserve) went to public school together, all primary grades in one room. In fact, for several years, Rose – who was herself only educated to the end of high school – taught all subjects, except French, at the one room school. Though some of her younger brothers were her students, according to family lore, she never had to discipline any of them with the strap, the infamous form of punishment in those days.

The class photo of 1930 says a lot. (See page 39). In it, no student smiled. No one donned new clothes. And not one kid was the least bit overweight.

The Jewish children attended an afternoon school beside the Sons of Israel synagogue to learn Hebrew and Jewish history. The synagogue itself ran strictly Orthodox services, but interestingly, not one single Jewish family from the Bay was very observant. Of the four-hundred attendees from all over the world who came to the reunion in 2001, my husband and I – and the last rabbi ever hired by the synagogue then laid off in 1962 – were the only ones who did not drive on the Sabbath. But, during the entire four-day event, only kosher food was served.

A funny story was going around that reunion weekend. Requests had come in from Sons of Israel synagogue in Sydney – about a 15 minute drive from Glace Bay – to join with the Sons of Israel in Glace Bay, the latter of which was soon closing due to falling membership. No way, said the remaining members in the Bay, none of whom were the least observant. No way would the failing Orthodox shul combine with the financially healthy reform synagogue from Sydney. Not a chance, even though the reform synagogue more reflected the values of the Bay congregants.

My cousin Dr. Stephen Cohen, who lives and works in Timmins, Ontario, had the good fortune to grow up in Glace Bay until he was twelve years old. He has some wonderful memories about Reserve too: "When the Cohen family first settled into the house in front of the small store in Reserve, it was across the street from the town's Catholic church. The priest told everyone that a nice Jewish family moved into the neighborhood and everyone should support them.

"Also, the Cohen family owned one of the first cars in Reserve and the boys were expected to drive anybody in an emergency to the hospital. Dad [that would be Louis Cohen] once drove a lady at double the speed to the hospital. She subsequently had triplets. Dad's major concerns were his having to deliver a baby and messing up the car."

As he also remembers, Sophie was deeply loved, by her children and grandchildren alike. "In my child's mind," says Stephen, "Bubby was there only for me. Much later I realized she was likewise centred in all the family's minds. Special in my mind is the memory of when a rooster jumped on my head. Bubby killed him and cooked him up for supper."

CHAPTER FIVE:
1941, A Year of Murder and Deadly Fire

As if the worsening war in Europe – and the much anticipated letters from family in Poland suddenly stopping – weren't stresses enough for Moishe and Sophie in 1941. They were about to experience two more harrowing ordeals: the brutal murders of Hyman and Rebecca Brody – Moishe's sister and his brother-in-law – in June 1941; and the fire on December 15 of that year at Mount Allison University in Sackville, New Brunswick, which killed four students and very nearly took the life of their youngest child, my father Goodman.

The murders shocked all of Cape Breton Island, indeed the entire province of Nova Scotia. The story of the Brody double murder is memorialized in the slow moving but beautifully enrapturing 1984 movie The Bay Boy, starring a most innocent, sweet and devout Catholic teenager, played by Kiefer Sutherland in his first ever feature movie. It won a Genie Award for best Canadian Film that year.

Filmed entirely in Cape Breton, and mostly in Glace Bay, the scenery – the vast ocean, the craggy shoreline and the cramped, wooden turn of the century homes – is intensely realistic and stunning. Though it does not primarily focus on the murders, and though certain artistic liberties are of course taken, the movie portrays how a loving and decent couple was gunned down in cold blood in their home. In the movie they are the "Silvers" and Sutherland, fighting his own horrors and emotional conflicts as a religious Catholic youth, is the sole witness of the crime, and terrified to come forward.

According to the booklet *Passage to Glace Bay: Our Ottawa Jewish Community Then & Now*, written for the 2001 Glace Bay reunion, the *Sydney Post Record's* announcement of the murders read: "Elderly Glace Bay Couple Are Victims of Brutal Slaying: Hyman Brody, who with his wife was brutally slain in his residence last evening, is believed to have been the dean of the Jewish colony of Glace Bay. During the last half century Mr. Brody became one of the town's most prominent merchants and real estate operators. With his wife he conducted a ladies' wear establishment on Commercial Street in the front of the same building in which he was so brutally slain Tuesday night."

Later on, the same *Post* article stated: The couple were regarded in all quarters as splendid citizens and expressions of horror were heard on all sides when it became known they were the victims of a fiendish murderer."

As it turned out, a deranged Glace Bay police sergeant had shot and killed the couple in their kitchen. The only living witness turned out to be an eighteen-year-old boy, who happened to be the son of another police officer. That officer was patrolling Commercial Street a short distance away when the crime occurred. The youth had seen Police Sergeant Arthur Frost – a Brody tenant who was months late with his rent – enter the Brody's home. Then the boy heard four or five shots before he saw Frost run away from the scene. He then saw Rebecca appear at the back door of her home, "screaming and bleeding profusely about her face," stated the newspaper. "She later re-entered the house, where she died from her injuries."

According to the Joe Brody eulogy given by movie producer Jon Avnet, Sergeant Frost was an anti-Semite and had access to the only gun in town, the one "used to shoot rabid dogs." He was eight months behind in his rent and the elderly Brodys told him to pay up or leave. This gave Frost the chance to put his latent plan into action. An ardent supporter of the Nazis, Frost believed it was only a matter of time before they attacked North America via Glace Bay. In those days, the idea that North America would fall prey to the enemy was not a totally ridiculous idea, given the progress the Germans were making throughout Europe.

Frost thought he would get a jump on the war in Canada by shooting his Glace Bay landlords. This would be his contribution to Hitler's cause. Frost was immediately caught, put on trial and found "overwhelmingly guilty," in Avnet's words. His sentence: hospitalization. He apparently suffered an epileptic seizure sometime in his life and he did, after all, have haemorrhoids. After a mere nine months in a prison-like hospital, he was released, free to live the rest of his long life relaxing in Glace Bay.

This travesty of justice affected members of the murdered couple's family in very different ways, most particularly Hyman's two sons, Moe and Joe, both dentists in New York at the time of the crime. They came home for the funeral, after which both left the mining town at the edge of the Atlantic Ocean forever. The victims were buried in the small Jewish cemetery in the middle of town, their resting places not far from that of Rebecca's father (who was my great grandfather) Yeheil Kekon.

The New York City dentists' long term reactions were as fundamentally different as could possibly be, and everyone in the extended family has always known this. As Jon Avnet described in the 1996 eulogy, "Somehow, Moe was never able to distance himself from the deaths of his parents and it haunted him throughout his life. They deprived him of the ability to experience much of the pleasure he deserved in life. Joe was quite the opposite and remarkable to a degree that few of us can find in anyone. [The murders] soured Moe Brody on life, for good reason, but somehow Joe remained resilient."

Joe never had any children, but he was gifted in every other aspect of life. He was large and strong. He had a fulfilling and successful career in dentistry in New York, the cultural centre of the world. He enjoyed two long and wonderful marriages. He traveled the world with his second wife, Ella. He casually conversed with Robert Redford and other Hollywood stars as he watched them make movies being produced by Avnet, Moe's son-in-law. He loved music and he painted. In fact, he painted, at age 93, a modern art portrait of my father Goodman as a mature man.

Visiting Joe Brody's apartment in New York in the 1960s and 1970s was like visiting Diana and Lionel Trilling's in the 1940s and 1950s. "It was a cultural meeting place for authors, poets and social critics," says my cousin Judy Kalin, who informs me that my father Goodman loved to spend hours and hours in Joe Brody's home whenever he could. "It was a parlour type apartment where intellectuals talked about world politics. It was very stimulating."

Joe even wrote a book, *A Man Called Joseph*, that his wife had published for him for his ninetieth birthday, five years before he died. The book tells many funny and exaggerated stories about his family and living in rural Nova Scotia. Among my favourite stories is the very first one, about his father Hyman's aging and beloved horse that was forced into hard labour by a demanding neighbour. The horse never forgave Hyman for caving in to the neighbour's aggressive insistence, and it died almost immediately upon being returned to its calm and pleasant pasture.

Disappointingly, and surprisingly, none of the chapters reveal anything about the murders of his parents or the author's feelings about them. The book is also silent about my own grandparents, who were, after all, Joe Brody's uncle and aunt who lived only one town over in Reserve.

The tragic dormitory fire came later the same year, in December 1941. My father, Goodman – by many accounts the smartest high school student in all of Nova Scotia in the late 1930s – was studying his first year away from home at Mount Allison University in Sackville, New Brunswick. In the wee hours of the morning on December 15, Goodman and his sleeping dormitory mates were awakened by a fire alarm and the screaming of others in the four-story residence. One of those others was Alex Cloville, one of Canada's finest and most famous artists, who was finishing his fourth and final year at the university.

Springing out of bed, Goody and his new university friends raced to the closest fourth floor stairway, but it was completely blocked by smoke. All the students on the highest floor went back to their rooms, slamming the doors behind them to give them more time to decide how to escape.

"I remember thinking, I am not going to die tonight," my father told me when I interviewed him about the fire for my magazine writing class in journalism school in 1983. Assigned to write a magazine style article about someone we admired, I could think of no one more appropriate than my father and nothing better to show what he was made of than the 1941 fire. Of course growing up I knew generally about the fire, as my mom would always refer to him as the hero of it whenever his back injury from that cold night flared up. But dad did not like to recall the details, so I needed to learn them by formally interviewing him for my assignment.

My father handed me a yellowed newspaper, *The Glace Bay News* section of the December 18, 1941, edition or the *Sydney Post-Record*. Its headlines announced: "Heroism of Goodman Cohen Praised By Youth: Reserve Youth Helped Companions to Safety; Eyewitness Relates Heroic Act of Goodman."

As the students began to panic, Goody kept his cool. He thought up the idea of tying all the bed sheets together to use as a rope to help the students lower themselves out the fourth floor window. This was hurriedly done under Goody's apparent calm supervision. When completed, the makeshift rope was anchored and hung out the window, and one by one the boys used it to escape. As leader, Goody had made sure the sheet rope was tied securely to a bed. He then helped hold it still while encouraging and assisting each boy through the window. When the second to last student was lowering himself, the rope broke, near the top as luck would have it.

Alone in the room, with no longer enough sheets or time to make another rope, Goody stared out the window to his friends on the ground, some seventy-five feet below. Already, dozens of other students had jumped from second and third story windows. Those on the ground had watched a boy too frightened to jump from the fourth floor become engulfed in flames. He was one of four students who ultimately died that night. Another student died of his injuries after finding the courage to make the jump from the top floor.

His friends were calling to Goodman to jump for his life. They had grabbed a blanket and were holding it out at each corner, like a circus net. Without much hesitation, but full of fear, he jumped. He fell through the freezing air with his eyes closed. Finally, he hit the edge of the blanket, bounced onto the hard ground, back first. He heard a crack, which happened to be his back breaking. He was required to spend a year in hospital in Sydney before returning to school.

There is no doubt that his brother Louis' decision to start a volunteer fire department in Reserve Mines had something to do with his youngest brother's near death experience in the fire that cold December night.

Taken in 1939 in Poland and sent to Sophie in Nova Scotia, from the European Weinberg family that would soon be wiped out by the Nazis. This is a picture of Sophie's mother, Mrs. Weinberg. I do not know her first name or age, but I do know she was religious. Notice the long skirt and her covered hair?

Sent to Canada from Poland in the 1930s, this photo is of one of Sophie's sisters, the sister's husband and their daughter, all names and ages unknown. Why include this photo then? Because they were part of my family, murdered by the Nazis. Like virtually all of my relatives, they were caring and honest. They did not deserve their brutal end.

Yeheil Kekon in his wedding picture. Taken in Russia, he dresses for the occasion and looks very serious, but if you look closely you can see there is a little glint in his eye. That is his dour sense of humour that he brought with him to Nova Scotia. This is the only photograph that I know exists of him, and it may indeed be the only one that does exist.

My beautiful great grandmother Raizel who died in Russia before her husband came to the New World. He waited to leave Russia, because he would never leave her alone. He had to stay with his sick wife until she no longer needed him. He brought this character trait – deep and abiding loyalty – to Canada; it was evident in all his children and grand children. Even profound unhappiness was not a reason to leave a spouse.

This is Sophie's wedding picture. The 19-year-year-old bride looks beautiful, for a 1906 wedding in Glace Bay, Nova Scotia. She is obviously nervous too, wondering if her husband will be kind and gentle.

Moishe Cohen's wedding photo. At 23, he is a handsome bridegroom indeed. Dressed in a three-piece dark suit, his shoes shined to glowing. He also looks a little nervous, as he waits for the ceremony and reception to be over so he can be alone with his gorgeous young bride.

Bessy Green on the left and Rose Green on the right, seated, 1915, Glace Bay, Nova Scotia. They are the children of Moishe Cohen's sister Fanny and her husband Bernard Green. Fanny and Bernard had the first Jewish wedding in Glace Bay. Their son Arthur, born in 1899, was the first Jewish child born in Glace Bay. Bernard was 20 years older than Fanny, and she gave him four children, including Bessie, born in 1908 and Rose, who was born in 1906. In this photo (which is also on the book's cover) the girls are seven and 10 years old respectively. If they are not the quintessential picture of beauty and innocence then nothing in my family's history is worth relating.

The back of the home in Reserve. The town's only general store was at the front. The Cohen family – initially and gradually increasing to nine members, and later and gradually in a declining number – lived in the house for about forty years. My Ottawa and New York cousins who spent summers there in the early 1950s remember a huge wood stove, a huge wooden table to seat more than 10 people, and a gramophone in the hallway. Chickens, cows and at least one horse shared the back yard.

This is the 1930 class picture from the one room schoolhouse in rural Nova Scotia. Notice the students, from kindergarten to grade eight, are not smiling, not at all over weight, and not dressed in expensive clothes. Goodman Cohen, no doubt the smartest of the group, is the sixth student from the left in the second row from the bottom. His oldest sister Rose taught in this school every subject except French.

Hyman Brody sports a moustache at the time this picture was taken, probably in the early 1930s. A successful businessman in Glace Bay, Nova Scotia, he owned property that he rented out and ran a general store. With his wife Chaya Baila, nee Kekon, they raised seven children. Hyman and Chaya Baila (who changed her name to Rebecca to sound more Canadian) were murdered by one of their tenants in June 1941 after they demanded he pay up his late rent.

Taken in the early 1950s during one of those idyllic summer vacations in Reserve Mines, in front of the Cohen house. Sophie is hugging her granddaughter Judy who is hugging her (Judy's) brother Howard, who is reaching down to pet one of Zaide Moishe's Collie dogs. Sophie has a bit of a smug look on her face, but why wouldn't she? Her adored children are starting to have families of their own, and she is very proud. She knows she did a great job raising a family in rural Nova Scotia.

Moishe and David Cohen. One of only two photos I have of my grandfather, this is taken outside the house in Reserve in about 1950. Both wearing ties, it could be the Sabbath, right before Moishe begins his five-mile walk to the Glace Bay synagogue. It's hard to read their faces, but they seem happy to be together. Dave is touching his father's shoulder, an intense show of affection for the Cohen men.

The burning dormitory at Mount Allison University in Sackville, New Brunswick, where four students lost their lives in December 1941, and where Goodman Cohen was a hero and badly injured.

All that was left of the Mount Allison boys' residence after the December 1941 fire that took four lives.

This is proof my father Goodman really was a hero in the deadly fire in Sackville, New Brunswick.

Goodman Cohen at 19 years old, with another injured student (in the hat), at the hospital in Sydney, Nova Scotia. This was 1942, a few months following the fire at Mount Allison University in Sackville, New Brunswick. They survived the December 1941 dormitory fire where four of their class mates died. Is that relief and gratitude in their faces? My father's back injury bothered him on and off for the rest of his life.

My dad's university graduation photo in 1947. Goodman Cohen: handsome, a young doctor-to-be and an eligible bachelor. He even had hair at that time! He was 25 years old.

Joe Cohen, 1927. This picture is taken around Joe's Bar Mitzvah. The shelves in the background are at Glace Bay's Sons of Israel synagogue, where he is attending for bar mitzvah lessons. It is not Saturday because no photographs could be taken during the Sabbath at the Orthodox shul. He already has that ruggedly handsome face that he would become well known for, at least among his family and friends.

Taken in Placentas, Cuba, around 1927, this is a photo of Gutman (the baby) and his parents, Clara and Jose Skrande. Clara was the daughter of Sophie's only brother, whose name and age are lost to history. As Sophie's niece, they wrote to each other constantly between Nova Scotia and Cuba, and despaired together through the mail when they both stopped getting letters from Europe in the early 1940s. The Skrandes loved Cuba, and had a hard time adjusting to America when they were forced to flee before Fidel Castro closed the border in the early 1960s.

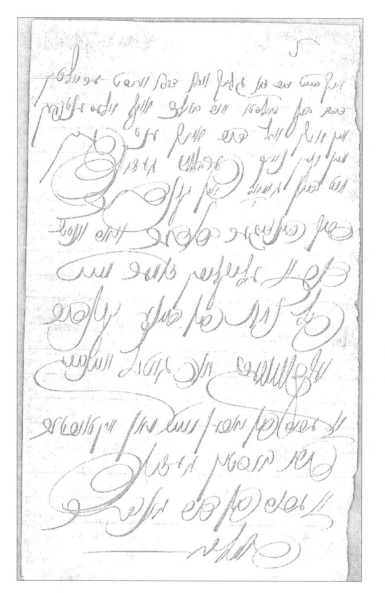

This is one page of the last letter ever received in Nova Scotia from family in Poland. Written in Yiddish, it discusses nothing about politics or the worsening situation in Europe.

Sophie and Joe Cohen in an Ottawa apartment, the one they lived in for a short time before moving to the place on the corner of Metcalfe Street and Gladstone Avenue. This photo of my grandmother and uncle was taken in February 1957, one month before my birth, and very soon after they moved from Reserve. Sophie knew she didn't have long to live at this point, and if she didn't get her remaining adult children out of Reserve, the tiny village in Nova Scotia where they had run a general store for some 40 years, Rose and Joe would never move themselves. Now in Ottawa, they were with five of the other Cohen siblings.

It is hard to say where this was taken, or exactly when. But, since it was a family shot, we do know it was after Uncle Joe died in 1969. Joe was the first to die, and these are the remaining six siblings. Back row, left to right, Goody, Sam and David Cohen. In front, left to right are Rose and Louis Cohen and Ethel Goodman. They look happy, as they almost always were when they were together.

Sophie in Ottawa in February 1957. To me, she looks strong, contented and relieved. After years of running a general store and raising a large family in Reserve Mines, Nova Scotia, she is ready to retire and relax. She doesn't get a long retirement, though; she dies the same year.

A beautiful photo of my New York relatives and my father in New York. From left to right. Eddie Goodman, Lottie Goodman, Eric Goodman, Ira Goodman, Ethel Goodman, and Goodman Cohen. Yes, my aunt Ethel married a man with the last name the same as my father's first name. We never got confused, but it made for some teasing. Eric is Lottie and Ira's son. The photo, taken at the Goodman's home, was snapped in 1986.

A treasured photograph taken in Ottawa at the Rideau View Golf and Country Club in the summer of 1990. These are all the living children of all the Reserve Mines Cohen siblings, celebrating the 25th wedding anniversary of Linda and Steven Weiner. In other words, we are first cousins. We had not all been together in one place since Michael Kalin's bar mitzvah in 1984, and we have not all been together in one place since. From left to right: Paul Goodman, Stanley Cohen, Adele Gottlieb, Lynne Cohen, Joel Cohen, Linda Weiner, Stephen Cohen, Judith Kalin, Barbara Cohen, Ira Goodman, Howard Cohen. Earlier that day, we had all been together at the Ottawa Jewish cemetery on Bank Street for my father's unveiling.

A 1982 photo of members of the family in Florida, where many of the
Cohens and their relatives – the Greens and Brodys – loved to go to escape
Canadian winters for at least a few weeks, or maybe a few months if retired.
They all look a little tanned, and well rested. Sitting, from left to right:
Minerva Cohen, Ann Green (Art Green's wife), Ella Brody, Sylvia Cohen,
Annie Green (Louis Green's second wife). Standing, from left to right:
Joe Brody, Arthur Green, Michael Kalin, Miriam Kalin, David Kalin,
Louis Green and Judith Kalin. This was taken at a family luncheon at the
Invernary Club House in Fort Lauderdale.

A treasured photo among the Cohen cousins, taken in 1968 at Agudath
Israel synagogue in Ottawa at Judy and David Kalin's wedding. From left
to right, the five brothers: Louis, Sam, Goodman, Joe and David Cohen.
Sisters Ethel Goodman (on the left) and Rose Cohen are sitting on the
bench. It's the only photograph of all the Cohen siblings that I am aware
of. They are thrilled to be together for such a joyous occasion. The only
thing I will add is that David (on the far right) lost a lot of weight soon
after this was taken and never put it on again.

Rita and Joannie Lambert are young teens in this picture. Rita is on the right, holding her white hat that she loved. They look happy together here, an unusual situation. The two often fought because Rita, older by a few years, was ordered by their mother to include Joannie in all her older sister activities. Rita resented what she felt were intrusions on her independence.

Katherine Lambert, my Nana Kay and my cousins' Kay Kay. She went to school in her forties – after her husband died and left the family penniless – to become a nurse's aide. In this photo, taken in Lowell, Mass., in the 1950s, Katherine is nearing retirement. I think she looks distinguished in her uniform, and the white shoes.

From left to right: Peggy Burns, Lynne Cohen and Nelson Burns. That is pain you see in my face. This photo was taken on or about June 14, 1985, a few days after my mother committed suicide. Aunt Peggy and Uncle Nelson flew up from Lowell, Massachusetts, so they could attend the funeral. This photo was taken by my then-husband Bill York, as we dropped the Burns off at the Ottawa airport on their way home. I was so torn up inside, I could barely think straight. It shows on my face.

Victor Lambert, not too long before he died in his 40s. This is the one and only picture I have of my mother's father. He looks happy because he is working at his piano bar, pouring drinks for customers and sharing a few laughs with his family.

My beautiful mother, Rita Mart Lambert, at her graduation from nursing school in Boston. She was a caring and compassionate nurse for years until she married and had children.

CHAPTER SIX:
Brothers and Sisters

As mentioned earlier, I gave a presentation on my family history for the Ottawa Jewish Historical Society in May 2010. Before I put that talk together, I wrote to all my cousins and my sister, and almost all of them – including my sister – sent me back the funniest and most heart warming stories about their Cohen-side parents, all of whom have passed away. In fact, only one spouse of the Cohen siblings – Minerva Cohen, Louis' wife – is still alive. What follows below is the second half of the presentation. (The first half was a twenty-five-minute summary of life in Glace Bay and Reserve, as well as a brief discussion of my family's Cuban connection). Given that the talk was formally focused on Ottawa, where six of the seven Cohen siblings settled, the following is also quite Ottawa-centric.

David Cohen

Though he was the second youngest, David Cohen, once he became an adult, was by far the leader of his family and the most influential in many of their life decisions, for example, on where they decided to live. His entire family – except his independently minded sister Ethel but including his resourceful mother Sophie – followed him to Ottawa.

Once they were all in Ottawa, the Cohen family was together as often as possible, especially on weekends. Dave's daughter Judy Kalin remembers the adult siblings getting together, "including with Sam and Sam's wife Sylvia, on Sunday nights. When dad's siblings Rosy and Joe moved to Ottawa from Reserve, everyone in the family met at their Gladstone Avenue apartment every Friday night. I remember the stale candies served at those gatherings. It was great growing up with a large extended family. I loved being with all my aunts and uncles and cousins. It was difficult for my mother, at times, because she felt that my dad spent so much time with his family and he was always including them in everything he did. Understandably, she sometimes wanted to be with him alone."

As much as any youngster in Reserve Mines, Dave could not wait to get out of the stifling rural town. Though he thought the United States was the greatest country, and though he often dreamed of settling somewhere south of the forty-ninth parallel, it seems events conspired to send him to and keep him in Ottawa. He first came to Ottawa in the late 1940s as a member of the Canadian Amy. He had never seen battle in Europe but that didn't stop him from being badly injured. He had an occupational accident: he fell through the roof of the Cattle Castle in Landsdowne Park. Now permanently injured, he left the army, and married an Ottawa girl – Queenie Levin – in a tiny ceremony. Then, he bought a small shoe store on Bank Street. Legend has it he was just driving by one day, saw a "for sale" sign and he bought the store. The rest, as they say, is history.

In his daughter Judy's words, "My father always worked in sales. He first owned two shoe stores, Vogue on Bank Street and Judy-Jay Shoes on Sparks Street. He later expanded the shoe stores and partnered with Sam to include three Ansony Shoes: on Rideau Street, Elmvale Acres and Hampton Park. My father was a very smart business person and always said that he would rather have gone into manufacturing shoes than sales. And he was way ahead of his time: Before big box stores, he always believed that he needed good stock to run a shoe store. My father always believed that self-service wholesale shoe stores were best."

What do we have today folks?

In Dave's later years he acquired a few properties with his brother Sam. These included the London Arms on Metcalfe Street – which they later sold – an apartment on Fifth Avenue, and an older, beautiful building on Echo Drive. My dad Goodman lived for several years at this last place, in the late 1970s after his separation from my mother Rita.

According to David's son Stanley, unlike his brothers, Dave was not an exceptional athlete. "Once when I was about eight or ten years old," says Stanley, "my bother Howard, dad and I were throwing around a baseball in front of the house. Dad slid and fell one time after lazily running. He exclaimed after getting up 'That's it. I've had enough.' He never came outside to throw with us again. Ever." However, it must be said that, contrary to the impression left by this story, Dave played hockey with the Glace Bay team, baseball with an Ottawa team in the early 1950s and later, he was a long time avid and successful golfer.

By any standard, Dave was an excellent employer. Some of his employees stayed with him for decades. They loved him and he loved them. He bought one of his workers a car as a gift after many years as his employee.

Which brings up another point: Uncle Dave was incredibly generous. He made sure all of his siblings who needed help were set up in businesses so they could be self-sufficient. He included Sam in many of his business transactions and was responsible for getting Sam the Metropolitan shoe store franchises in both the Sparks and Rideau Street locations. When my dad Goodman and Rita settled in Ottawa to be near dad's siblings, Uncle Dave bought my parents their first car, and their first TV. That sturdy TV lasted almost 20 years. It provided years of entertainments as it sat in our play room until the mid-1970s.

Says daughter Judy: "He was very close to his siblings and would do anything for them. When he traveled, which was not often, he would include them, usually taking Sam and Sylvia and Ethel and Eddie." When Goody was dying of prostate cancer in 1989, Dave took him on his last road trip through New England.

Dave could not do enough for the people he loved. Judy says: "He was a good, loving father and grandfather. When my daughter Miriam was 12 months old and hospitalized at the Children's Hospital of Eastern Ontario for a dislocated hip, he was heart broken and would visit with her every day, just sitting by her bedside. He didn't want to leave. I believe that he was with her more than I, her mother, was. When Dave's siblings died, their children, his nieces and nephews, became his children too."

It's funny that Uncle Dave couldn't wait to get out of Reserve, because once he had kids of his own, he was determined that they spend weeks there every summer for years. In other words, you could take the boy out of Reserve, but you couldn't take Reserve out of the boy. My cousin Judy tells the cutest and funniest stories about her memories of Reserve: "Every summer until I went to camp at seven years old, my father and sometimes my mother would take me and my brother Howard to spend a few weeks at the home in Reserve Mines. Those are the best memories, when my brother Howard and I and my cousins, Ira, Paul, Stephen, Joel and Linda would spend part of the summers playing in the Nova Scotia town. The old house seemed gigantic but when I visited it in later years it was actually pretty small. The front part of the house was the store, which at that time was being run by my dad's brother Joe and his sister Rosy. I'll never forget the potato sticks. We were allowed to choose something from the store and the salty potato sticks were delicious.

"We spent our days at the park, playing and picking blueberries. Linda and I were especially close. I remember my grandmother, Sophie, plucking feathers from the chickens. There was a chicken house, and a horse or two. We kids would collect eggs. I have no memories of my grandfather, Moishe, as I was too young. But I well remember that Uncle Sam would give me a penny for every grey hair I would pull from his head. I was not too keen on this game. But those were wonderful times."

Dave was not much of a disciplinarian. His son Stanley explains it this way: "When I was about ten or twelve, a police officer rang our door bell. He was responding to a complaint by a neighbor about me throwing snowballs. I was terrified when I saw this giant police officer step inside and ask to speak to a parent. I woke Dad up from his usual evening nap. He and I stood there listening to the cop giving a stern lecture. Then dad said to him, and I paraphrase, 'Where did you learn to speak like this? You must have had good training!' The officer looked stunned and muttered 'never mind how I sound. You need to speak to your son.' After the cop left I lay quietly on the carpet near dad, waiting for the punishment. Guess what? He never said a word and fell back asleep."

Like my father Goody – indeed all the Cohen siblings – my Uncle Dave had no strong religious feeling for much of his life. After he got married, he did not keep kosher. He wanted his kids to experience Christmas, so every Christmas Day he took the three of them to the home of one of his long time employees, Mrs. Hicks, where she always had several gifts for the kids. One year, Dave put up a Hanukkah bush at home. Of course Dave's family also celebrated Jewish holidays, usually with Queenie's sister's family. Then when Sophie died in 1957, for a year Dave said *Kaddish*, a prayer recited every day for an extended period during synagogue services by mourners after the death of a close relative. From then, he became a little more interested in Jewish life.

The main turning point for him was when he and Queenie visited Israel in 1967. He became a strong advocate for the state. He supported the Jewish National Fund and other organizations financially. In later years, he was very happy to be in Florida during the Christmas holiday season, as he came to dislike that time of year. Indeed, he loved the Jewish life in Florida. When his daughter Judy married David Kalin and started keeping a kosher house and observing all the Jewish holidays completely, Dave loved participating. He even came full circle and kept a kosher kitchen in Florida so the Kalins could visit comfortably.

Even before he was mildly religious, Dave was incredibly wise. As patriarch of the family, with the patience of Job, and never, ever complaining, Dave understood long before self-help was popular that a positive attitude was everything in life, and he led by example. Everyone in the family went to Dave for advice on finances and lots of other issues, and almost always he was right.

One last thing about Uncle Dave. As mentioned, he was a golf enthusiast for many years. He played virtually every day at the Rideau View Gold Club right into his eighties. Indeed, as he aged, as long as he was golfing, his entire family knew he was healthy and happy.

Rose and Joe Cohen

I am discussing these siblings together rather than individually because, though neither of them ever married, and though Rosy was the dictionary definition of spinster, they were like a married couple in many ways. Indeed, they are even buried beside one another at the Ottawa Jewish Cemetery on Bank Street. Back in Reserve, as Sophie was aging and her health was failing, she realized that she had to move to Ottawa, and take Rose and Joe with her. She knew if she died in Reserve, those two would never leave the rural town. So, Sophie closed up and sold the store in Reserve and the three of them, with lots of help from Uncle Dave, moved – after a very brief time in one small downtown apartment – into the apartment on the northeast corner of Gladstone and Metcalfe. The three of them lived there till they each died: Sophie in 1957, Joe in 1969 and Rosy, after some 35 years in the same apartment, in 1990.

My cousin Joel tells me Rosy and Joe almost never talked. "Joe was crusty," Joel says, "and he'd make a face behind her back whenever Rosy talked. But Rosy was always happy, always pleasant. I'd say she was even cute."

Rosy looked after Joe's health, injecting him with his needed insulin every day. She also complained quite constantly about Joe to her other siblings.

According to my cousin Stephen Cohen, "Joe was a trucker for awhile in Nova Scotia and a great bridge player when he came to Ottawa, but really he was a home town boy with health problems."

Joe not only had diabetes, he suffered with scoliosis and he was quite stooped over. I remember little about Joe as I was twelve when he died. But I am proud of him for a few reasons. Joe – who, according to Stephen, was handsome, smart, kind, funny and warm, as well as life master bridge player – decided not to marry *because* of his health problems. According to Goody, he did not want to burden a wife. So he chose to be single. I think that was noble.

With his brother Sam, Joe played bridge a few nights weekly, and they travelled to play too. They were both life masters. Based on tournament points, this designation by the American Bridge League is no small feat. At that time, the rank was the highest any bridge player could achieve.

Joe was quiet, especially if Rosy was around. This may hearken back to rural Nova Scotia, where Rosy taught in the one room school house he attended. Remember Rosy's qualification for teaching school was that she finished high school. So she taught most of her siblings, which may explain why some of them never went much beyond primary school. According to Stephen Cohen, Rosy also played piano at social dances above the Brody's store in Glace Bay. I'm pretty sure she was home by the time the Saturday night fights broke out.

Rosy tended to talk non-stop. In the words of Ethel's son Ira: "Rosy was different from the other Cohens. She was very outspoken and a strict disciplinarian. We now know she wasn't really that way, but that's the impression she gave."

She read every newspaper she could get her hands on, and would clip out items if she thought one of her brother's might be interested in them. Hilariously, she talked about cooking and recipes all the time, but she never cooked. This was irritating to Dave's wife Queenie and to my mother Rita too. Not only did she never cook, but Rosy was extremely thin because she was too cheap to eat. When Rosy moved to Ottawa, her sister Ethel would cook up a storm – mainly chicken – for whenever she came to visit from New York, so Rosy would have some home cooked meals.

Rosy loved being with people. When she and Joe had the shoe store on Elgin Street – set up for them by their younger brother Dave – for about ten years, she really loved interacting with all the customers and window shoppers who came in, just as she had while working in the store in Reserve. The Ottawa store was right beside the Mayflower Restaurant on Elgin and Cooper Streets. Rosy and Joe schmoozed a lot with Ernie Potechin who worked nearby. Conveniently, both Rose and Joe walked to and from work every day.

As Ethel's daughter-in-law Lois Goodman writes: "Rosy brought some of Reserve Mines to the shoe store she ran in downtown Ottawa. I was quite surprised when I visited Ottawa to see a big barrel with a checkerboard on it when I entered the shoe store."

Being a miser, Rose never got her drivers license, so she walked just about everywhere. Daily, even in her eighties, she walked from her apartment on Gladstone to the Loblaws grocery store on Catherine Street where she bought bread and vegetables that were old and on sale.

Did I mention Rosy was a miser? To a degree most people will never see, and for no apparent reason – as she always had enough, even growing up in Reserve – Rosy never spent a dime she didn't absolutely need to spend. She never took a bus, let alone a cab. Indeed, Dave bought her first television for her. Later her brothers together bought her a color television in the late 1980s. It was even later than that that they had to buy her a window air conditioner because she would never buy one for herself. She must have survived on less than $10,000 a year, but when she died, she still had every penny her parents left her, which had increased exponentially through Rosy's savvy investments.

Due to Sophie's insistence, Rosy sent every niece and nephew – all twelve of us – ten dollars and a card on our birthdays, even after we were married with our own children.

Don't get me wrong. Rosy may have been cheap, but Rosy cared deeply about her growing family of nieces and nephews, and their children. And we all loved her dearly. Like her mother before her writing to her cousin in Cuba, Rosy wrote constantly to her sister Ethel in New York City. Rosy always had a letter out on her little phone table in the process of being written. It got mailed once a week. Long distance phone calls almost never happened because they were too expensive. The letters were so important: both sisters never tired of hearing about what everyone in the family was doing.

Being older, she was like a grandmother to me and my sister and brother. We visited almost every Sunday, and our reward was a Hershey's chocolate kiss. Judy remembers her family picking up Rose on Sundays for a drive around Ottawa later in the day.

Rose loved to be invited for dinner and her relatives were always amazed at how much she could eat, as she was very thin. No doubt she was starving herself most of the time. Ethel shopped for clothes in New York for Rosy and sent them by mail. Rosy never bought anything for herself. She wore the same dresses – never pants – for fifty years! It drove Dave and Goody nuts.

Ethel Goodman

My cousins Ira and Paul and their wives – though they never lived in Ottawa – were about the most prolific writers when I asked for information on their parent Ethel. I couldn't leave her out just because she didn't settle in Ottawa with all her siblings, and I wouldn't want to. She was resourceful and loving, and never stopped caring deeply for her growing Ottawa family. She married Eddie Goodman, a New Yorker, and settled there to raise her two boys. I will let them tell you about her.

Ira wrote to me: "Mom decided neither Reserve nor Glace Bay were for her so she packed up after graduating high school and relocated to Brooklyn. She lived with Lena Rakowsky." Remember Lena? She came to Canada from Russia with her dad, my great grandfather Yeheil, and moved to New York City almost immediately to live with an older sibling. "As a single woman," Ira continues, "Ethel worked as a secretary and a bookkeeper, but once she married in 1939, she settled in as a homemaker, and she was a very good one. Mom was, like all the Cohens, very family oriented and close to her siblings. She wrote to Rosy every week, and always looked forward to getting her letter from Ottawa. Frugal as they were, telephone calls were out of the question. Mom really missed Rosy and her letters after she died. But she was never one to dwell on sadness and any mourning that she did was strictly private."

Ira Goodman recalls those summers in Nova Scotia: "Every summer till I was twelve, my mother, my brother Paul and I went to Reserve Mines for three or four weeks. We travelled there to be with Judy and Howard and our other cousins. My father couldn't go because he had the automotive store in New York and there was no one else to manage it. Those years and visits to Reserve were really special to a city kid who never saw a farm, much less a general store. Our hosts were Grammy and Pop, as we called them, along with Rosy and Joe. At that time, Rosy was a school teacher and Joe minded the store. Joe knew where every item in the store was and he was liked by all of the customers. It's funny the things I remember about the store. I remember the smell of fresh oranges each wrapped in green paper, and how I'd have one every morning. We'd have just-picked eggs, because they also had a farm behind the house, with a horse, a few cows and a lot of chickens. The store had heavenly chocolate milk in glass bottles. Actually all drinks were in glass bottles. I can't remember the name of the chocolate milk but I had a few every day."

Ethel always loved her siblings and wanted to be with them as much as possible. When some of the Cohens became snowbirds and travelled to Florida every winter, "my parents also bought a condo in Lauderdale Lakes just so they could be together with everyone," says Ira. "Mom was a just a wonderful person, kind, smart, talented and loving. She was the mother everyone wants to have. She was a super cook and homemaker. Like the other Cohens, she was into physical fitness, walking a few miles every day to one of the neighborhood shopping malls in Queens. When grocery shopping, she'd bring along her cart. Also like her siblings, she was pretty frugal. In fact no one could stretch a buck like mom."

Wait a minute Ira, what about Aunt Rose?

He goes on: "Dad, being a New Yorker, was a very hard worker, running the auto store six days a week. On his day off, he'd wash the car and we'd go for our Sunday spin. This is how it was in the 1950s. It was good. We lived well, did well in school and were fortunate to have the opportunities we had. We moved into out first house in Floral Park in 1955. This was true suburbia, and it was great: drive-ins, roller skating waitresses, American Band Stand. Take me back!"

Ira adds: "Growing up with large families on both sides was a blessing, but I don't think we appreciated it at the time. Large families are not very popular now. When you asked about the family there was always something to say. So many aunts, uncles and cousins. And such warm, nice people, (pretty smart too). It was great.

"I really miss those days spending time with our extended family, catching up on everyone's lives. As is always the case when the former generation passes on, the current generation loses touch and doesn't have the time or the interest to be as close as our parents were."

Though born and raised in Canada, Ethel became as American as apple pie, even throwing huge Fourth of July barbeques that became famous in her Queens neighbourhood. And interestingly, one of her sons, Paul, did at one time think of moving to Ottawa. In 1969, as Rosy was retiring from the shoe store on Elgin Street, Paul thought he might take it over. As his wife Lois explains: "I researched Canada. Then I traveled alone to Ottawa to stay with Rosy and house hunt. What a trip! Eddie and Ethel drove me to the airport. Ethel gave me a plaid, fabric suitcase filled with frozen food to bring to Rosy. In those days you had to change planes in Montreal and wait two hours. David and Queenie and Rosy met me at the Ottawa airport about eleven p.m., but my luggage had not made the trip. I was frantic. Of course, David took over dealing with the paperwork, and then he took Rosy and me back to Rosy's apartment where I would be staying during my visit. Rosy gave me a nightgown and I slept in a bed with beautiful, lace edged linens. About three o'clock in the morning we were awakened by a knock at the door. An airline rep was there with my luggage, including the plaid suitcase. He knew it was the correct suitcase as it was wet from the defrosting food."

Lois continues: "I'll never forget that trip as I got to know the Cohen branch of the family. Sam generously loaned me his car. I learned that a gallon in Canada is not the same a gallon in the U.S. And I began house hunting and price checking baby food. I went out to a family cabin on a lake where cousins Freddie and Deli Gotlieb were staying. Freddy caught a huge fish which he later cooked up. It was the best, and freshest, fish I'd ever eaten. Deli took me house hunting. Queenie had me over to dinner. She taught me how to steep tea.

"Houses within our price range were about fifteen minutes away from the store. The Ottawa Cohens tried to tell me that it was too far away." That was probably because, in their hearts, they still lived in Reseve Mines, where commuting to work was not an issue at all.

Lois continues: "In New York I was traveling forty-five minutes to work, so fifteen minutes was very close as far as I was concerned. I fell in love with the Ottawa family during that trip. Paul eventually joined me to look over the house I'd found and talk business. Goody saw how lonesome I was for my baby, especially on Mother's Day; this was my first child. I called home from Goody's house and spoke to my seven month old baby who could say a very intelligent 'goo-goo, gaga.' Everyone was kind and generous to me. We ended up not moving to Ottawa, but we came close, having filled out much of the paperwork to emigrate.

"My mother-in-law Ethel was a wonderful cook and a wonderful person. She taught by example, never interfering, but always there for her children when needed. She showed her love through food. Paul and I still call toasted rye bread comfort food. Her sliced meat was amazing, as were all her dishes, including chicken soup, which was heavenly. I'll never forget the first time Paul brought me over to meet his family. I wore my new camelhair skirt and a matching blouse bought just for the occasion. I made sure my hair and makeup were just right, and was extremely nervous. When Ethel opened the door she greeted me warmly and welcomed me with a hug and kiss. My nervousness disappeared. Dinner was a loud, funny and happy occasion. The family told jokes and didn't discuss serious matters, unlike my super serious family. This was wonderful to me. I fell in love with the family and couldn't wait to call Ethel and Eddie Mom and Dad, which I did as soon as Paul and I officially became engaged."

Sam Cohen

Sam Cohen was a good looking man, very handsome. According to his son Joel, "he was the most handsome of the Cohen boys, and he kept more of his hair than any of them. He had a little bit of hair on top of his head. Sam was movie star good looking."

But Joel has no idea what place his dad came in the age order of the Cohen siblings: "That would have meant we had to talk," says Joel. "If it isn't obvious by now, let me spell it out: The Cohen men did not talk much at all. The Cohen male line was a very strong male line, but not particularly communicative."

But they all worked very hard, Sam no exception. "My dad was a hard working guy," says Joel. "He came up to Ottawa at Dave's behest, and worked with Dave in the shoe business.

"There was an opportunity to have the shoe concession at the Metropolitan store on Sparks in 1950. So we came up from Brooklyn. I was born in the Brooklyn Jewish Hospital. In New York, Sam ran a fruit and vegetable store on Washington Avenue during the depression. His partner embezzled from him. So my family came up here. I was six years old when we came to Ottawa. We first lived at 36 Russel Avenue in Sandy Hill. Then we moved around the corner to 261 Laurier Avenue and we stayed there for many years. The street cars stopped right in front of our apartment.

"We never owned a home, but it was a nice apartment, a lovely apartment – three bedrooms. We had a den, with a Lay-Z-Boy. My mom Sylvia was not the greatest cook in the world but she made pies well.

"My father eventually took over the second Metropolitan shoe store on Rideau Street. And there was also the Sony shoe stores, one at the corner of Rideau and Nicholas, one at Hampton Park Plaza and one at Elmvale Acres. My dad was in partnership with Dave in all these stores.

"They also invested in bowling alleys and in other property. They invested in Hampton Park Lanes and Kent Lanes. Our cousins Steve and Linda Weiner took over the bowling allies when Louis and Minerva retired. They also invested in real estate together. They bought the London Arms on Metcalfe, with the whole family. It was sold many years ago to

John Toth, whose family owned Dworkin Furs. Then Dave and my dad bought that beautiful apartment on Echo Drive, around 1970.

"My dad never bought a family home, but he drove really nice cars. He always drove beautiful, late model cars, *which sat in the garage.* Like most of the Cohens, my dad was a walker. Remember, the famous thing about our grandfather was that he walked to synagogue from Reserve to Glace Bay and back on Saturdays. It must have taken him hours.

"Like Dave, Sam did not finish high school. He left Reserve when he was sixteen. He went to New York and stayed with his Aunt Lena. While there he was a messenger for a while. He met my mom in New York. They were probably fixed up. My mom was from Newark, New Jersey. She was a secretary for awhile. They married in New York City and settled there and that is where Deli and I both were born, she in 1939.

"Sam didn't serve in the army because he had flat feet. We all have flat feet. Even I do. My feet are like boards. We all wear orthotics."

"Sam was a tease. He teased my mom. Sam had a sense of humor, but he did not have a smile that you could not get off his face. He was not that kind of guy. He was a bit of a whiner."

Sam was deeply loved by Uncle Dave, says Dave's youngest Stanley. "Even though Sam seemed a bit sour at times, the two got along fabulously. I never heard Dad say a bad word about Sam. Perhaps, my most cherished memory of Sam was the day I drove Sam and Sylvia to New York City shortly after I got my license. I can't remember the occasion. I was behind the wheel of Sam's beautiful car. At one point Sam and Sylvia were sitting in the back arguing loudly about something stupid. Just then I pulled 'a fast one' to get through traffic by successfully jumping a median. After that, they sat there quietly cuddling each other and never muttering another bad word for the rest of that trip!"

Louis Cohen

In a letter from my cousin Dr. Stephen Cohen, who lives in Timmins, Ontario, this is the story of my Uncle Louis: "Louis was born May 3, 1912. From that moment on, my dad was always on the go go go and he lived life to the top. He loved all sports, especially tennis, and he played hockey for a Cape Breton Island team. After we moved to Ottawa he went on to become the largest bowling operator in the city. He designed, patented and sold the right to a bowling ball machine which he called the KONY. He ran bowling leagues, and every year he hosted large banquets at major Ottawa hotels, including the Skyline on Lyon Street. These banquets included up to twelve-hundred guests, addresses by the mayor of Ottawa, and lots of hoopla by the Ottawa Roughrider cheerleaders, major prizes as well as local singers and musicians. Louis was a people person, and with tongue in cheek he often referred to himself as Mr. Bowling."

Louis married Minerva in the early 1940s. How did they meet? Says Stephen: "In 1942, in Glace Bay, my mother Minerva was invited to visit a girlfriend, Bessie Tannenbaum, who was a sister to Dr. Arthur Green, a well known general practitioner in Glace Bay and a first cousin to our fathers. Dad was there visiting too, and the two were introduced. It was fireworks after that, lucky for me and my sister Linda.

"In Reserve Mines, dad was a volunteer fireman and a search and rescue operator. When I was in medical school, I asked him about his resuscitation of a person found frozen to death. He said he gave him a few slaps across the face. Louis could be a card, to use the language of the times.

"My parents had a general store called the Black and White located in the rough area in Glace Bay, known as the Hub. Credit was the norm as everyone was living pay check to pay check. How could you refuse food to customers who suddenly had no job or money? By 1955 our business died with the coal economy when natural gas came in from Alberta. Actually, it was a blessing in disguise because it brought us to Ottawa where my both my parents' families were. My parents built a new business in bowling. I went to medical school and we had the comfort of being near both sides of our family.

"My parents were totally devoted to each other. I have never seen them argue, fight or act out in a way that made me think less of them. Sometimes I have thought it left me stupid and naïve in certain ways because I always expected the best in people. They complimented the differences in each others personalities, but they had the same character: both were good people."

Goody Cohen

As noted above, Goodman was the favourite of everyone in the family. As the last baby, he was adored by all. As a young student, he was constantly praised for being exceptionally smart. When he went through McGill medical school in the 1940s, he got so much money from his family that he never had to work while in university. Goodman was the only Cohen sibling to attend post secondary school.

Unlike his brothers, thankfully, my dad loved to talk about Reserve. He regaled his children with lots of stories about growing up in small town Nova Scotia, like how he pitched baseball for the local team and how, for the briefest time, thought of doing it full time. He often talked about his parents, and how their division of labour was so unfair to his mother, whom he adored. Though he held his dad in some contempt for his constant reading and studying Jewish law in the ancient languages, Goody did like to brag about how Moishe taught himself English from reading newspapers. And he was proud that my grandfather did influence him to learn vocabulary at a young age by reading the sports pages.

My father was the only sibling to marry a non-Jew. My mom Rita was a nurse from Lowell, Massachusetts. The two met at the Massachusetts General Hospital in 1952 and had a civil marriage in Maryland in 1954.

He lied to his mother and sister Rose, telling them that Rita was "half Jewish." But once everyone was settling in Ottawa and his own mother was dying, my father and mother decided they had better make good on their lies. They went to Montreal in February 1957 – one month before my birth and with my older brother Martin crawling at their feet – and my mom and brother converted to Judaism. My parents also remarried at that time in a religious ceremony.

In 1967, when I was ten, my mom and dad answered the first call for members of Temple Israel, the reform congregation in Ottawa. Our family attended there infrequently for about eight years, after which my parents separated and later divorced. They were the first couple to divorce in our family.

My dad was one of the first cardiologists in Ottawa. At the Ottawa Civic Hospital he treated thousands of satisfied patients over thirty-six years. My sister Barb and I are blessed to still encounter people in our city who remember him with great fondness.

I will let my cousin Stanley and my sister Barb relate their memories of him.

Dave and Goody were always close, and when their youngest kids, Barb and Stanley, were still young, they found an activity for the four of them. I'm pretty sure they thought that by bringing their youngest children for these outings, their rowdy behaviour would never become public. But Goody and Dave never considered Stanley writing about these ventures for this Ottawa Jewish Historical Society talk. Okay, the two men weren't exactly out of control, but for Cohens, they were absolutely wild.

"Dad and Goody took me and Barb to Jarry Park in Montreal to watch baseball several times in the early 1970s," says Stanley. "On the way in the car, they spoke about all kinds of normal things but as soon as we arrived it was all baseball. They especially loved it when the public address announcer called out the players' names, like Cocoa

Laboy and John Bacabella – 'Baucckh-ah-bellllla!' – which Dave and Goody repeated loudly and in unison. Their favorite of course was the red-headed superstar Rusty Staub. When Rusty would come up to bat they cheered him on to hit a homer and when he did they stood and cheered like kids. Dave would even try to whistle, but it came out pretty weak. The popcorn calls were mostly made by Goody. I clearly remember the times he would yell for the aisle boy to 'throw four popcorns up here.' In a way, that was the highlight catch of the night for me and Barb. He would proudly stand and snatch bags out of thin air thrown by the confection boy standing several rows down. He'd do a one handed catch for each of us. The nearby fans would get a big kick out of this."

Stanley continues: "My Dad adored your dad and loved to discuss practically any subject with him. But my fondest memories truly were going to Jarry Park, just the two dads and me and Barb in the back seat. They absolutely loved baseball."

My sister Barb remembers working for Goody for a summer in his medical office, and she feels very sorry for his secretary Sharon Edelson to this day. "Poor Sharon," she says. "I was a partying little demon and hated working. But I remember how incredibly wonderful dad was with his patients who constantly commented on how much they loved him. One man told me 'your father is a miracle worker who has finally given me relief from my pain.' I will never forget this man.

"One day, I'm not sure why, but I didn't notice that a patient was in the waiting room. Dad had no patients in the examining room and was actually waiting for the guy who was in the waiting room. It was probably ten complete minutes before I noticed the patient. Dad was so upset, and I was mortified. Goody just couldn't stand to keep patients waiting. There is no question he sacrificed income because of this conviction.

"By the end of the summer, I must say, I felt totally inept. I was young and immature and remember constantly disappointing dad and Sharon. That part need not go in your talk." Woops! Sorry Barb.

Stephen Cohen also has something to say on Goody: "He was like a mentor to me during medical school, and I owe him a lot of unsaid thanks for my career."

CHAPTER SEVEN:
Lowell and All the Ladies

Leaving aside my father's family for the moment, my mother's family is about as different from his as apples are to pitted cherries. For one thing, Rita Mary Lambert was born into a family of devout Catholics, Irish Catholics to be precise. She grew up in the town of Lowell, Massachusetts – population today just over 100,000 – about forty minutes northwest of Boston.

Though small, Lowell is, in fact, considered the "cradle of the American Industrial Revolution." Why? Because it was the original American factory town on a large scale. Textiles were its manufacturing base, and textile mills – and the livelihoods they offered – are what attracted immigrants from all over Europe, especially Ireland, to Lowell. Though currently reconstructed into a quaint tourist city of historical interest, Lowell continues to struggle with the loss of industrialization as a mainstay of the American economy.

My mother's maternal grandparents sailed as teens or very young adults – like my paternal relatives, on a Cunard Line or Allen ship – from Dublin, Ireland, in the late 1800s, across the Atlantic directly to Boston, after which they took a train to Lowell.

Though they left years after the Irish Potato Famine (1845-1852), their emigration can certainly be considered part of the mass exodus that directly resulted from it, and that saw upwards of two million people swarm to the U.S., Canada, Australia and other parts of Europe.

Mary and Dennis didn't come to Lowell together. Mary Hart came first, arriving in Boston at age seventeen with her aunt, and very few belongings. Her boyfriend back in Ireland could not bare life without her, so Dennis O'Neill took a Boston-bound steamship two years later. Dennis came with his two brothers and his sister Katie.

The first chance he got, he married Mary in a tiny Catholic church on the mill town's main street.

Dennis and Mary, like all new European immigrants, came wanting a better life. They were attracted to Lowell – the "town of canals" near the Merrimack River – because of its dozens of towering textile mills and the jobs they offered. Dennis worked as an oiler. His job was to lubricate the massive machines that kept the mills running. This was not a safe job. But he was careful, and was able to raise his big family on the salary he earned.

As observant Catholics, the O'Neills had many children, nine in all, counting Dennis Jr. who was born second but who died at three years of age. Katherine, my grandmother, was the oldest, born in 1905, and obviously named after her father's sister. John was third. Then came May, then Lawrence, then Margaret (or Peggy), Steven, Emmett, and finally Eileen. From all accounts, they were a close family. According to Peggy, they all died in their seventies, except May, who died at eighty-four, and of course Peggy herself who, in 2011, is ninety-seven.

Peggy – who spent a long career as a public health nurse – was my mother's favourite aunt and my grandmother Katherine's best friend and sister for 73 years until Katherine died in 1978. Peggy is still living in her own condominium just outside Lowell with the younger of her two sons, Larry. Her doting daughter Mary-Jane visits every day. In 2008 Peggy told me that the longer she lives, the more she misses her brothers and sisters, especially Kay "who was a saint."

Mary Hart was the matriarch of the O'Neills, a family dominated by women both in numbers and in personalities. An excellent cook, she gave many of the women in her family – my mom and I included – their "big" genes. Mary was usually forty to seventy pounds over weight, even when she was young. It didn't bother her in the least. She was always happy and frequently laughing. Indeed, she was known for her joyous sense of humour. Her exuberant attitude was infectious. My mom Rita adored her, and often recalled her grandmother's hearty laugh. In fact, my mother inherited Mary's laugh and great sense of humour, but she never came to terms with her "big" genes, like her grandmother did. Rita spent much of her adult life on one diet or another.

Peggy reports that her parents Mary and Dennis enjoyed socializing and playing cards with their many friends and neighbours. "They all took turns hosting game nights," she said, "while we kids looked after ourselves and babysat our younger siblings and our parents' friends' children. It was always lots of fun."

Mary's oldest child, my grandmother Katherine, always received the highest grades in her classes, including at high school and later when she returned to school to become a nurse's aide. She was known to everyone as Kay. My siblings and I lovingly called her Nana Kay. Her Lowell grandchildren called her Kay Kay. We saw Nana Kay about once a year when she visited our home in Ottawa, Ontario. Nana Kay *always* brought presents for me, my brother Martin and my sister Barb. We always enjoyed her quirky choices for gifts. During the week-long visits, she enjoyed smoking cigarettes with my mom while they sat in the family room and gossiped for hours about the family in Lowell.

Returning to the past, Kay married Victor Lambert when they were both eighteen in about 1923. They had two children two years apart: first my mother, Rita, born November 22, 1928, then Joannie, born March 1, 1930. Victor, who came from an even larger family than his wife, was the son of French Catholic Canadian immigrants, a group that made up another large contingent of Lowell residents at the time. They came to the city for the same reason everyone else did in those days: to work in the textile mills. It is rumoured that Victor – who tragically died in his forties of a heart attack, leaving his small family flat broke – spoke French. My late mother never told me this, but my aunt Joannie – who currently has some dementia and is living in a nursing home in Lowell– seems to think he did. This fact is odd because my mom never knew more than *bon jour* and *bon soir*. But then again, her dad was not around much. He was, by any definition, an absentee parent.

Victor Lambert had a gregarious personality, and my mother adored him. He loved to drink alcohol and may very well have been an alcoholic. Like many children of alcoholics, Rita remembered her remote father as the wonderful parent, and her mother as the strict, unfair and unloving disciplinarian.

Though his parents and siblings worked in the mills, Victor never wanted to, so he tried other things. For some years he supported his family by working as a chauffeur. By driving around local big wigs, he earned enough to rent a small apartment and put food on the table. But he lost this job during the depression. As my mother used to say, during hard times, the first victims of budget cuts of wealthy employers are always going to be the drivers.

Victor was down but not out. In 1930, he realized he could support his family and his own habit by selling illegal booze. He became a bootlegger, and a damn good one at that, only spending about two months in prison before Prohibition ended in 1933. After that, he went straight and borrowed the money to open a piano bar in downtown Lowell.

Joannie – who married the adoring and devoted Frank Tully – tells me she remembers visiting the bar as among her fondest memories. Rita also loved the bar and being out with her parents, especially finally getting to spend "quality" time with her father. In fact, according to Aunt Joannie, the whole family being together in the bar was among the happiest times for Kay and Victor also.

Growing up sheltered in tiny Lowell, brilliant, gorgeous and outgoing Rita and her somewhat less resourceful younger sister Joannie – who with Frank raised two devoted and successful children, Ellen and Steven -- did everything Catholic. They attended mass every Sunday with their mother. They associated with only Catholic friends. They abstained from meat and only ate fish on Fridays. And they only attended Catholic schools – right up through grade twelve – where they were often taught by nuns. When I was growing up, Rita used to refer to Sister Mary Alison as her all-time favourite teacher. This grade eight maven instilled in Rita a life-long love of history, particularly American history.

Nana Kay – who my mother always claimed loved her (my mother) more than she loved Joannie – was very strict, demanding the girls frequently attend mass even during the week in the mornings before school, and that they give up their favourite hobbies for Lent. Rita annually gave up reading, which she loved even more than movies.

Both girls were forbidden to date boys or smoke cigarettes until they were twenty-one years old. Thus, on my mother's twenty-first birthday – on November 22, 1949 – while she was on a date for her special party, she bought her first pack of cigarettes. From that moment, Rita chain smoked until she committed suicide 35 years later.

The two girls did all the cleaning and laundry for the family, but for some reason none of the cooking. Doing these household chores when she was young – from changing all the sheets every week and doing all the laundry to scrubbing the floors – may have been what influenced my mother to despise housework as an adult. She blamed her lifelong guilt for hating and avoiding housework on being Catholic while growing up.

At least she ended up loving to cook – "though," she often said, "cooking every day takes the joy out of it." For decades after my mother's 1954 civil marriage to my dad, she suffered for housework twice: first, over her sometimes unclean, untidy home; and secondly over the guilt of not working to change it. But however bad she felt, she could never bring herself to admit that housework was in any way important.

Because of the restrictions placed on her by her strict mother, who forced her to take Joannie everywhere from the library to the Christmas concert, Rita grew up hating her mother and resenting her younger sister. According to later tales, she only loved the father she almost never saw. He was like the saviour who never really saved her.

Victor died young, when he was in his early forties, of cardiac arrest. Rita was nineteen and in nursing school in Boston, while Joannie was only seventeen. For the rest of her life, irregularly, Rita dreamed of her adored father, always waking up in tears.

After Victor died, Nana Kay did something seemingly very brave, but in some ways very selfish. Middle aged, she enrolled at the Tewksbury State Hospital to become a nursing assistant or, what is called in Massachusetts, a licensed practical nurse. She stayed in a dorm room at the hospital while she went to classes and earned her LPN. All her needs were met. But in the process of looking after herself, Nana Kay basically abandoned her two daughters. For Rita, who was being boarded at a hospital in Boston while she earned her RN, it might not have been too difficult. But Joannie of course found it very hard to be on her own, and she understandably resented her mother for years.

Kay worked as a LPN for about twenty years. With the little amount she earned, she was able to support herself in a small apartment. My father Goodman subsidized her income with several hundred dollars every month, which – according to Nana Kay's beloved sister Peggy – allowed my grandmother to go to Florida every winter when she retired. She always stayed in a rented trailer there, and enjoyed the warmth and sun.

I don't personally remember anything negative about my Nana Kay, though my mom often said negative things about her as I grew up. Indeed, she said she hated her as a girl, and therefore, as a girl and young adult, so did I. Now, I am left with painful and longing feelings almost every time I think about Nana Kay. I have unfinished business with her. I never said good bye, and the last time I saw her I do not remember being at all loving towards her.

At the time, I was an immature, loud mouthed nineteen-year-old know-it-all. I was living with a thirty-one-year-old man on a farm south of Ottawa, on the outside of a small town. Nana Kay came for her last visit to Canada and was staying at Rita's new Kanata townhouse, a home she had bought in the summer of 1977, about two years after my parents' separation. She had invited me and my boyfriend over for dinner one night while Nana Kay was visiting. So we all gathered – including my sister Barb, who still lived with mom – at the Kanata home for a meal.

After my boyfriend and I left for the farm, my mother told me a week or so later, Nana Kay expressed concern about me "living with that old guy." I never saw or spoke to Nana Kay again. She died the following summer. Her worry was not for nothing. On the way home that very night after dinner, he and I had a fight. He kicked the steering wheel while I was driving, and we drove off the road into a ditch about a mile from the farm house. We walked home and called a neighbour, who used his tractor to pull my car out of the ditch in the middle of the night. I continued to live with this man for months afterwards.

Funny, my Aunt Peggy, Nana Kay's sister and closest friend for life, often refers to her sister as a saint. Indeed, Peggy becomes teary eyed when she mentions Kay's name. It seems sometimes as if Nana Kay was two different people. Peggy says Kay was incapable of being mean to anyone, or of even having a negative thought. Kay favouring one daughter over the other? Not possible, says Peggy. According to one of Aunt Joannie's children, my cousin Ellen Nutter, Kay Kay was to be feared. Aunt Joannie confirms this. Though Kay outwardly favoured Rita, according to Joannie, she apparently beat up her older daughter as much as she physically abused her younger one when they were children and teens. After Rita married and moved to Canada, Kay Kay still frightened Joannie and her kids, though no longer in a physical way.

In her later years, Rita's infrequent trips home to Lowell always followed the same routine. As a last minute decision, she would phone her Aunt Peggy to say she was coming. Then she would get up the next morning at five a.m. and start driving. She would drive for nine hours straight, arriving in Lowell around two p.m. By then, everyone knew she was coming, and they were giddy with anticipation. Her cousins loved her, and Aunt Peggy went into overdrive. Staying with Peggy and her husband Nelson Burns, Rita would excitedly visit her cousins and other relatives, who would usually organize an impromptu party. Rita was so fun to be with. Rita was so funny. Rita was so hip. Rumors have it she even smoked dope with some of her younger cousins.

Nana Kay died in the summer of 1978. As the daughters, of course Rita and Joannie inherited everything Kay owned, which was very little. Being the magnanimous wealthy sister, Rita told Joannie she could have everything. When Joannie arrived at Kay's apartment after the funeral, some of her many female relatives were busy trying on Kay's clothes and going through Kay's things. This obviously upset Joannie, who clearly deserved more respect after her mother's death. She was rightfully angry. A rift in the family was created that did not heal until my mother's death in 1985.

In 1986, my sister Barbara and I went to visit our Lowell relatives. Of course this included our Aunt Joannie. That was the end of the family rift. From that day, for more than twenty years, Peggy started to call and visit Joannie regularly. According to Joannie's daughter Ellen, to whom I have been close since about 2001, Peggy has been a godsend since Joannie entered a Lowell nursing home. Until Peggy broke her hip in 2007, she was visiting Joannie minimum once a week.

In 2007, while Joannie was living in a nursing home, Uncle Frank was recovering in a nearby seniors' home from seven brain surgeries. He still loved his wife as if they were honeymooners.

As part of her job as a nurse at Massachusetts General Hospital – even at that time one the most reputable hospitals in the world – Rita, twenty-two years old at the time, took blood for the Red Cross. In 1952, one of her blood donor patients happened to notice her natural beauty and charming laughter. He asked her out to dinner. She accepted. Nurse meets doctor. Goodman Cohen meets Rita Mary Lambert.

They married two years later in a civil ceremony in Maryland. No guests. No flowers. Not a single photograph commemorates the occasion. In 1957, they married again in Montreal, this time in a religious ceremony following Rita's and my brother Martin's conversion to Judaism. Again, no guests, no photographs.

Who would have such a barren wedding, let alone a second, matching sterile affair? For some strange reason, I am proud of my parents for being so completely different from everyone else on this issue. It didn't bother them, and, compared to some, their marriage was pretty darn good, at least until they separated twenty two years later and then divorced about ten years after that, a huge, egregious mistake in my never-to-be humble opinion.

Furthermore, nothing shaped me emotionally or intellectually more than this divorce, not my brother's suicide when he was nineteen years old, not my mother's suicide when she was fifty six. But all of that is for a different family story at a different time. It will no doubt take me a few years to write it, but of course it will be worth the wait.

CONCLUSION

It might seem difficult to go from basically reciting family history to analyzing the disparate facts and coming up with a coherent conclusion. But it actually is not that hard. As with many Jewish families, survivorship resonates throughout our history. But I also see other threads in the lives of my recent ancestors from Russia to Poland to Ireland to Lowell to Cuba to Reserve Mines to Glace Bay to New York City and to Ottawa. As this quick and heart-felt history has shown, my family is infused with many positive and substantial character traits, among them: courage, gratitude, physical and moral strength, generosity, common sense, loyalty, humor and intelligence. When I dig very, very deep, I can even see tiny glimpses of these characteristics in me, qualities I dearly hope are being passed on to my children and my grandchildren.

Unlike today, it was fairly normal one hundred years ago for a person to need to use their G-d-given traits to survive. Today it is much easier to get away with not needing – indeed, to get away with living an entire life without using – faith or strength or courage or generosity, or even gratitude. Ten or twelve decades ago, it took a good dose of backbone, self-confidence, gumption, and sturdiness for my family – for any family – to leave Europe with little money and to come to the New World.

Then, married couples almost invariably raised large families with not much more than hope and trust in G-d that their children would have bright futures. Today, even many religious families restrict the number of children they have because of the financial burden twenty years hence of university and weddings. What a difference in perspective!

One hundred years ago, when big families were the norm, the benefits were obvious. Not only did the parents have at least several strong, sturdy and stable adults to care for them in their old age. Large families also guaranteed years of liveliness – entertainment if you will – and they created close ties among lots of siblings for lifetimes. My family, on both sides, was no exception.

These days, many members of the Jewish community are often cynical, and for lots of genuine reasons. Centuries of hatred and anti-Semitism will do that to a group. Non-Jews aren't exempt: today, everyone seems at least a little sardonic and contemptuous. Even the Cohen and Lambert cousins – including myself – have adopted a little modern acerbic skepticism in our personalities But such attitudes were absent in the older relatives on either side of my family.

Why? The reigning trait in their hearts and minds as they matured must have been primarily gratitude: grateful to make it to the Atlantic shore safely; grateful to find a warm bed for the night; grateful to get that job or to be able to buy workable property; grateful to find a decent spouse; to have another healthy baby in bed at home; to be healthy enough to have another baby when one died; grateful that the bills got paid, that the murderer got caught; that he survived the fire.

When my family came to the New World seeking betterment, they took nothing, and no one, for granted, not their coal mining customers in Glace Bay and Reserve, not the hard driving textile mill bosses, not the lowly mill workers who became their friends in Lowell. And certainly not the close relationships in the large families they created.

Death does pack a wallop. The murders of my great aunt and uncle, in the middle of the worst Holocaust mankind has ever inflicted, has I am sure left all of their progeny with lingering tensions, whether we recognize it or not. And more than ninety-five years after Dennis Jr. died of natural causes at age three, my Great Aunt Peggy still mentions her older brother in any conversations about her nine siblings. And she never met him!

My wonderful European ancestors came to North America to find better lives. They were fortunate, and so we are fortunate. They have not only given me – and hopefully all my remaining family – the ability to look back with love and gratitude, but also with a sense of humor, and a very large dose of satisfaction.

THE END

ACKNOWLEDGEMENTS

My acknowledgements, very simply, include my family, my friends, my publisher and G-d. This work would never have even started were it not for my first cousin Judy Kalin and her husband Dr. David Kalin. Together, they created a huge family tree in 1984 that described crucial details of our recent ancestors, details that allowed me to begin this project. And every project needs a beginning. I would never have started this work if they had not laid that ground work. Moreover, Judy scrutinized my work – both the book and the Ottawa Jewish Historical Society presentation – several times.

I want to thank Elaine Brodsky of the OJHS. As my neighbor and close friend, we sometimes walk to synagogue together on Saturday morning. One day during that walk in 2007 I was telling her about my family research. She suggested I give a talk on the subject for the OJHS. I am so grateful she suggested the idea then encouraged me to carry through with it. I also want to thank my cousins – as well as my sister – who sent me anecdotes and information about their parents for the OJHS presentation, that I finally gave in May 2010. That information, included in this book, allowed me to bring our family's history closer to the present, so we can sense a little bit of Reserve Mines in all of us.

Many of my friends have been supportive as I worked on this book for the last four years, but no one as much as Brian Hanington, an international businessman, speaker and published author. Once my rough draft was completed, Brian took the time to thoroughly read it, critique it and guide me right through to the finish line. I owe Brian my first born, but she won't go.

Thank- you to Trafford Publishing for creating a beautiful product, and for not raising your self-publishing rates until after we signed our contract. A special thank-you to Trafford's Nika Corales, Nina Olmedo and Kyle Anderson for handling my project personally and doing so with kindness and calmness.

And thank-you Joseph Ben-Ami, my wonderful, patient husband and brilliant amateur historian who put up with me, encouraged me and loved me all the way through to the end.

Chibalaya

Patricia Brody

This I told you:
School was not for girls.
My mother – who was she – let me carry
my basket filled with fresh eggs to the goyim.
I was maybe ten, near Minsk. I made money.

1.
I had no given name, that luxe-custom
of the New World of which I am not truly
I am not Betsy, Rivka or Chibalaya
paying my all-night ride,
leaving my brood of six.
Yes, I opened my front door – did I have a choice? –
but not my arms
to the poor half-wit Chaim brought.
He never said a word from over sea.
Five hundred dollars he had in his pocket
and this little secret,
five hundred dollars, he came calling.
He was meant to marry Fannie, then saw me.

2.

He was meant to marry Fannie, then saw me,
I had no given name,
Rivka or Chibalaya, she must have named me
something at my birth.
It snowed who was my mother?
All night I rode who am I,
I sat up on the board-bench in the train;
for my comfort I would never slip a penny,
I had to stay awake
lest the shysters and paskutzva touch my dress.
Did I smell of my chickens and my cows
of my youngest child, Selig,
crying, still wrapped-up in his mama's bed?

3.

Crying, underneath my layers
my crumbling silk
black with coal and Selly's tears, he could still smell milk;
I sat up all night, the locomotive chugging
south from Halifax to Orchard Street.
The money from my eggs sewn in my slip,
the cream and butter of my toil and sweat
and I bought cloth: foulard, lawn, worsted,
hats, garters, stockings, linens, girdles,
and where I stayed — Delancey Street, whose house?
Then the journey back, two nights again
sitting up, the dry-goods for my pillow,
the child sobbed they said, that whole week
without me.

4.

Curled in my feather bed without me,
he grew wary; wary he would stay.
For the first time we had money.
We bought a building, there's a sign
marks the alley. Chaim tried to make a club
for dancing.
It was in the finest house
death came calling, whiskey on its breath;
did my foolish man sell the stuff
that killed us? Copp-er-man, face like beets
yeah, far from his green home he was,
full of rage and rye –
No Jew would bother him again, he screamed.

5.

My boy – they spat on him, Jew – weeping,
stained my silk black sleeve,
I'd no choice but to open up my door,
though not my heart, to that simple-simon girl
your pa brought me from over icy sea.
His from Gott knows what lost barn-hour
rolling in the rotted Russian hay.
Here we lived, shivering in Glace Bay,
kinder rode on glaciers, scorned the snow.
Lily, Esther, Joe, you left us and we
perished in the kitchen, where candles burned
on Shabbat. Rafe, Moishe, Selly
I meant to scream, the bullets tore me near in half
I alone tried crawling for the door

6.

My blood on fire they found me by the door
No Yid would get the best of him, he swore.
Never did I lie in my own room
sea breeze at the glass, sun on my clean muslin
fresh water in the basin
     a jar for my ashes.
They let him off you bet;
who should pay for two Yids shot to bits?
Chaim fell before me.
     I had a comb
my hair pulled back and tight,
my daughters gone to Calgary,
so far they went to marry.
In my wedding photo,
my cheekbones shine in the light.
Serious, I clasp your father's shoulder.
Närish boy was s'posed to marry Fannie, but got me.

7.

On the floor, he got me. Of course they let him off.
All of you came weeping to the trial.
Rarely did we talk of love   your loss,
you all did good for me,
better than your papa,
I wanted…

Now we lie freezing in this ground,
the blackened stars, the airless mines shut down.

      I crawled to earth
our gravestone smashed blanked out,
who's to guard this corner of the graveyard?
They shoveled us like coal into the dirt
cold we are cold
until our blood runs out

8.
I tried to scream the blood filled my mouth
they pushed us in the ground
the sky winged with violet smoke
and gold and
coal-blue dusk
I could not look up
I had to stay awake!
My youngest saw the ocean from my window
the wind-hurled green, this north Atlantic hole
I never touched it
      did I smell the salt?
Fridays, I would bake the sweetest brot,
braided gold, the challah for my blessing.
Other nights was "Soup again?" and you all cried for challah…
My own eggs gave the bread that pretty color.

Chibalaya (Chaya Baila) Kekon married Chaim (Hyman) Brody in 1894. They settled in Glace Bay, Nova Scotia, a coal-mining town. She bore six children and raised a seventh, Molly, who was reportedly her husband's child from a previous marriage. Using money she saved from selling home-grown dairy products, she opened a women's/children's dry-goods store. All of her children worked in the store and the business thrived. In June, 1941 Chibalaya, 67, and Chaim, 77, were torture-murdered by a policeman to whom they rented a room. Although the officer was brought to trial for the murder, he received an inadequate sentence.

Permission to re-publish this poem was granted by the Manhatten-based literary magazine *Big City Lit* and the author.

This poem was published previously by *Poet Lore*.

Poem-Eulogy for funeral of Martin Cohen, April 16, 1975
By Rabbi Jerry Steinberg. Printed here with his permission.

I know Martin
    Do you?
He's the lad who strums a guitar
And sings of a life he doesn't understand
Yes, he's the young man who asks questions
    That no one can answer
    Because he sees things that others don't

Martin – Martin embarrasses me
    Demanding more than I can give
    Ands he makes me feel inadequate
    For I can't even give myself some of these things
    The hope of a future for all men
    The promise of love in spite of all
    The peace of knowing my own soul
    The strength of self-respect, of saying I matter
    The joy of knowing that when the sun rises tomorrow
    A few more people will see it.

Martin – You pain me
    For all this and more you've asked of me
    Yet I didn't quite make it with you

I guess wrapped in my own cacophony of sound
I didn't hear you as I should have
As I would have liked to
Yet I tried
As did others
I cared and I loved
And what I couldn't accept in you
    Was really what I couldn't accept in myself

I guess Martin, what I am saying
    Is that I am very human
And I thank you
    For teaching me about myself.